On Your Bike

OXFORDSHIRE

Ellen Lee & John Broughton

COUNTRYSIDE BOOKS

NEWBURY BERKSHIRE

COUNTRYSIDE BOOKS
3 Catherine Road
Newbury, Berkshire

To view our complete range of books,
please visit us at
www.countrysidebooks.co.uk

ISBN 978 1 84674 229 3

Photographs by Ellen Lee
Maps by Gelder design and mapping

Cover photograph supplied by Derek Forss

Designed by Peter Davies, Nautilus Design
Produced through MRM Associates Ltd., Reading
Typeset by CJWT Solutions, St Helens
Printed in India

CONTENTS

AREA MAP SHOWING THE LOCATIONS OF THE RIDES

INTRODUCTION

Cycling is much more than a way of getting from A to B. Journeying by car, bus or train you exist in a state of limbo, places rushing past too fast to experience them and only the start and destination having any solid reality. By bicycle, travelling becomes a complete sensory experience. You see, hear, smell and sometimes even touch your environment. You travel slowly enough to interact with your surroundings, to wave a greeting, to exchange a smile and to see those small details which help define each place as unique. Yet you travel quickly enough to see the subtle changes in land use, architecture and contours which mark out one area from the next.

All the rides or at least part of them are in Oxfordshire which, as we hope you will find, is still a varied and pleasant place to cycle. The scenery you will encounter as you ride the routes changes enormously, from the gentle floodplain of the River Thames to the hilly uplands of the Cotswolds, from the former fenland of Otmoor to the chalky downs of White Horse Hill. Everywhere the present landscape is very much influenced by the past and it is impossible not to feel the history as you ride along.

The routes vary in distance from 6½ to 29 miles and even with visits to places of interest and stops for refreshment none should take more than five hours to complete. We have tried to indicate what sort of terrain you should expect. Don't be put off by a few hills. They add a different sense of perspective and none are too steep or too long.

Cycling is what you want it to be. Whether you like to ride on your own or with friends or family, or whether you enjoy riding fast, savouring the physical pleasures of riding or you prefer to potter around in a more leisurely fashion, stopping en route to investigate nooks and crannies and savour the sights, sounds and tastes of the country … whatever and however you do it, we hope that this book and its suggested routes inspire you with a taste for bicycle adventures.

Ellen Lee and John Broughton

GUIDE TO USING THIS BOOK

This section is aimed at cyclists who have not ventured out on a touring ride before. It is important to go prepared so that if a problem occurs you are in a good position to cope with it. Firstly, make sure that your bicycle is in a roadworthy condition. Check the tyres for wear, or damage, and make sure that they are properly inflated. Check the brakes. Change badly-worn blocks. Treat your bicycle as a friend and it will reward you with many miles of happy cycling.

Having made sure that your bicycle is well looked after, it is time to attend to your needs. Make sure that your bicycle is adjusted to suit you, as a wrongly adjusted machine can be very tiring and uncomfortable. If cycling alone, the confidence and knowledge of how to deal with a puncture will bring peace of mind.

Always cycle in comfortable clothing and go prepared with some waterproof clothing, even if you think you won't need it. If cycling in the winter, take an extra layer of warm clothing as well, just in case the temperature drops unexpectedly. It is a good idea to carry a drink (water will do) and a snack to fend off thirst and

hunger. Water bottle carriers can be fitted to any bicycle.

Other things to carry with you should include a basic tool kit, puncture outfit, tyre levers and a spare inner tube, not forgetting a suitable pump. Most experienced cyclists change the inner tube if they have a puncture as it is easier than mending the puncture on the road. Another reason for carrying a spare tube is that a puncture can occur in a place where it is not possible to stick on a patch.

TIP: *Make sure that your tool kit contains a pair of long-nosed pliers which are very useful for pulling out thorns, etc. when they have caused a puncture.*

SAFETY

In general when cycling on a public highway obey the Highway Code, and use common sense. The wearing of helmets is not compulsory in the UK and is left to the discretion of the rider. It is a good idea to wear something light in colour so that other road users can see you. Remember that it is the responsibility of the cyclist to make him or herself visible, especially in low light.

Secret Oxford, Streams, Islands and Fishes

10 or 8 miles

Although this route starts and finishes in the heart of Oxford, it explores many of the less well-known but nevertheless fascinating faces of this university city. Even if you are Oxford born and bred, there will probably be a few roads and tracks you didn't know existed. Beginning by heading south and west alongside the river to Osney Island, we then continue through parkland and along paths to the village of North Hinksey, where you can enjoy a well deserved refreshment stop at the Fishes, a popular stream-side pub, or just enjoy the stone and thatch cottages in this pleasant village. We return via the hamlet of Binsey, Port Meadow and finally the Edwardian academic suburban dream of North Oxford.

Map: OS Landranger 164 Oxford, Chipping Norton and Bicester (GR SP516063).

Starting point: Radcliffe Square, just north of High Street in the centre of Oxford. If you are driving there, it is strongly recommended that you use one of the town's Park and Ride sites as parking in the city centre is limited. Seacourt Park and Ride on Oxford's western side (GR 491064) is the closest to the city centre. Oxford's railway station is located about ½ mile west of the city centre.

Refreshments: Oxford itself caters for all budgets and tastes. Along the route we suggest trying the Fishes at North Hinksey or the Perch in Binsey. Port Meadow is a pleasant place for a picnic and to watch boating activity of all kinds. If you're riding as a family, it's also a good place to get off and stretch your legs and let the children have a good run around!

The route: This 10-mile route starts in Radcliffe Square and heads south-west using mostly river towpath and cycle tracks, and despite being a city-based ride, it uses almost exclusively cycle tracks and minor roads. It is therefore a particularly family-friendly ride. You can shorten the route by 2 miles by missing out North Hinksey.

Start from the eastern side of Radcliffe Square with the Radcliffe Camera to your right and All Souls College to your left. Ride out in a southerly direction. Cross High Street at the pedestrian lights. **Turn R** and immediately **turn L** down the narrow, partly-cobbled Magpie Lane. **Bear R** at the junction (Merton Street) and soon **bear R** into Oriel Square. **Turn L** through bollards onto Bear Lane and **bear L** into Blue Boar Street. The Museum of Oxford is

To Wolvercote

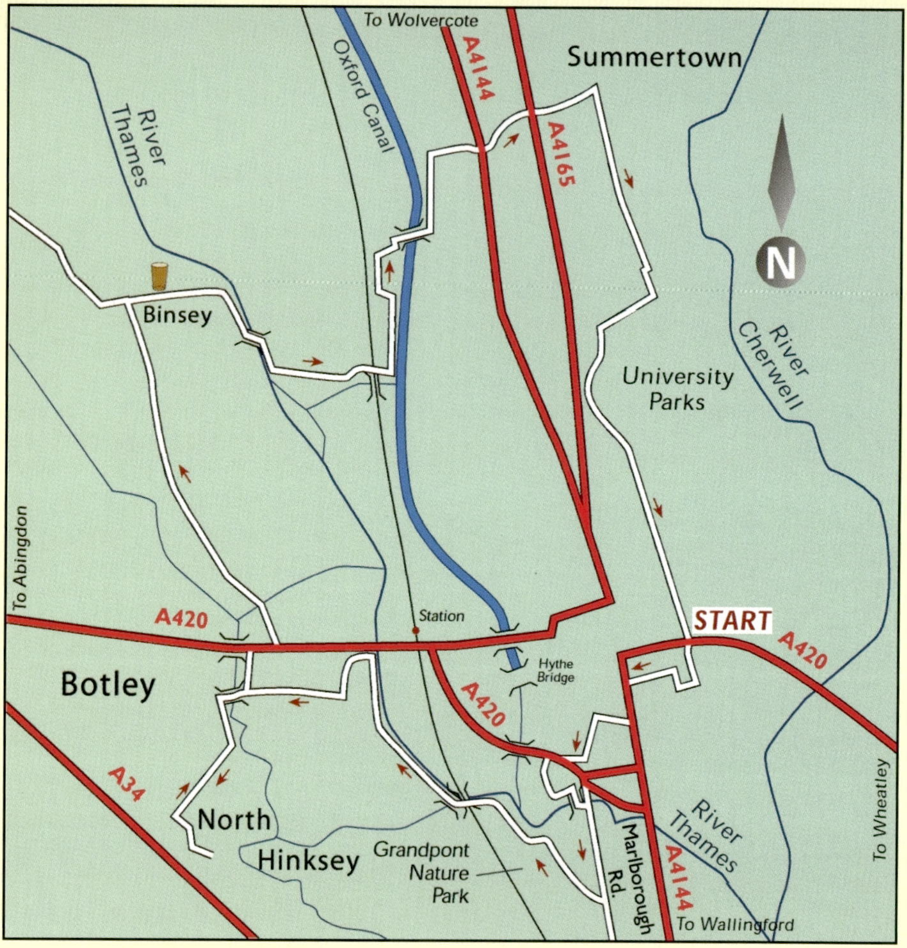

Summertown

A4144

A4165

Oxford Canal

River Thames

N

River Cherwell

Binsey

University Parks

To Abingdon

A420

Station

START

A420

Hythe Bridge

Botley

A34

A420

North Hinksey

Grandpont Nature Park

Marlborough Rd.

River Thames

A4144

To Wheatley

To Wallingford

located at the T-junction with St Aldates. **Turn L** and pass the main entrance to Christchurch College on your left. **Turn R** soon onto Brewer Street. Take care as this is a little difficult to spot. If you find yourself at the traffic lights with Speedwell Street, you have gone too far!

Pass the entrance to Campion Hall (the University's only Jesuit College) and **turn L** at the T-junction (Littlegate Street). **Turn R** on the left-hand bend and soon **turn L** onto a cycle track

(marked Routes 5 and 7). Follow the track **R** onto Thames Street and cross at the pedestrian lights. Keep following the Route 5 and 7 signs onto Blackfriars Road, Trinity Street and Friars Wharf. Cross the River Thames on the foot/cycle bridge. On exiting the bridge, **turn R** (river on left) and soon **turn R** onto Marlborough Road. **Turn R** at the crossroads (Whitehouse Road). Ride to the end of this road and **turn L** onto a gravel track through Grandpont Nature Park. Follow the track as it passes under the railway bridge and

Port Meadow on a sunny afternoon

onto the riverside path. Dismount and push your bike across Osney Lock.

You are now on Osney Island and therefore surrounded by water! Soon go ahead onto East Street with the Watermans Arms pub on your left and the river to your right. At the end **bear L** down North Street. Go straight over at the crossroads onto West Street. **Turn R** (Swan Street) and cross the bridge over the stream and ride carefully along the cycle track as it goes around the edge of a school. Keep a good look-out for pedestrians and fellow cyclists as the path is narrow and twisty. Cross Ferry Hinksey Road using the pedestrian lights and go straight over onto the path along the edge of Oatlands Road Recreation Ground. Keep a look out on your right

for the end of Riverside Road, the last terrace end you pass before the path bends left to cross a wooden bridge over the stream. If you don't want to go on to North Hinksey and instead shorten the route by 2 miles, then follow the tarmac path onto Riverside Road and continue the route at (*).

Otherwise, follow the path over the wooden bridge and **bear L** where the path forks shortly after. **Turn R** at the T-junction with the tarmac cycle track. This is Willow Walk. Ride over the stone bridge and soon **turn L** onto the road in North Hinksey. **Turn L** by the church down the no through road (signed The Fishes Public House). You will find the popular stream-side pub about 100 yards down the road on your left.

When you are refreshed and have taken the time to enjoy the pleasant stone and thatch cottages opposite, retrace your steps. Ride back down Willow Walk and **turn L** onto the cycle track through the field, over the wooden bridge and follow the tarmac side track to the left onto Riverside Road.

(*) Cross Botley Road using the traffic island (CARE!) and **turn R** onto the pavement cycle track for a short distance. **Turn L** (Binsey Lane). After approximately 1 mile, and in Binsey village, **turn R** through a kissing gate (signed Bossom's Boatyard). **Bear R** at the river and keep to the track nearest the river. Cross at the red arched footbridge and continue on the other side, soon **bearing** L up the ramp and across the wooden plank bridge. Keep straight ahead along the stony track and exit Port Meadow through double green gates.

Keep straight ahead and cross the railway. **Turn L** at the T-junction (Rutherway). **Turn L** (Merrivale Square) and soon **turn L** (Plater Drive). At the second sharp right-hand bend, keep straight on onto the cycle track and through two sets of metal bollards. **Turn R** and go straight over at the traffic lights at the canal bridge. **Turn L** (Hayfield Road) and **turn R** at the crossroads (Frenchay Road). At the end of the road, **turn R** onto the pavement cycle track and cross Woodstock Road at the pedestrian lights. **Turn R** and immediately **turn L** (Staverton Road). Once again **turn R** onto the cycle track at the end of the road and cross Banbury Road at the pedestrian lights. Go straight ahead onto Belbroughton Road. **Turn R** at the T-junction (Charlbury Road). Go straight over the

crossroads (Linton Road) and then straight over the next crossroads onto Dragon Lane (past the Dragon School). Exit through the gate and **turn R** and immediately **turn L** (Fyfield Road). Turn R (Crick Road), **turn L** at the T-junction (Bradmore Road) and **turn R** at the T-junction (Norham Gardens). This whole area was built in the Edwardian era, when University dons were first allowed to marry and needed houses befitting this new status. Few dons could afford these grand town houses these days!

Turn L at the T-junction onto a gravel cycle track alongside the University Park and University Museum of Natural History. At the end of the track, rejoin Parks Road. Go straight over at the traffic lights and continue on to the next traffic lights. Go straight over onto Catte Street and continue back onto Radcliffe Square and the end of the ride.

• •

OXFORD
When you are on High Street, you are in the centre of the city. Make sure you have some time to explore. The University consists of about 35 colleges, each of which is a separate and self-governing institution. The colleges vary greatly in age and in character. Some of them open their grounds free to visitors. Look out for notices in the porters' lodges. Just off to the north of High Street is Radcliffe Square enclosed by the University Church, Brasenose and All Souls Colleges and the Bodleian Library buildings. In its centre stands the Radcliffe Camera, one of several reading rooms of the Bodleian Library.

The Ashmolean Museum (the oldest public museum in the country) houses art

and artefacts from all around the world. There is also the University Museum of Natural History, a wonderful example of Victorian public building design; the History of Science Museum (the original site of the Ashmolean collection); the Pitt Rivers Museum (anthropology); the Museum of Oxford; and the Modern Art Museum, so something for everyone.

PORT MEADOW

There is a (probably) apocryphal story about an American visitor to Oxford who asked a history professor to show him Oxford's most ancient monument. The professor took him to Port Meadow on the north-western edge of the city. Evidence of occupation of this large area of floodplain meadow goes back to the late Neolithic and early Bronze Age (2200–1700 BC). Aerial photographs show round barrows enclosed by ditches, some of which were clearly visible on the ground up to the 1940s when they were excavated. They proved to be high status inhumation burials of the so-called Beaker People, whose grave goods included characteristically decorated pots. Studies of ancient pollen from the meadow have demonstrated how agricultural activities intensified in the area during the Iron Age, with much greater emphasis on keeping animals.

Today Port Meadow is enjoyed by the inhabitants of Oxford in many ways, for walking, sailing, flying kites and in particularly hard winters, skating. The area is also designated as an area of special scientific interest because it supports several rare plants and huge flocks of wading birds, especially lapwings and golden plovers in the winter.

Oxford Heights and Otmoor

7½, 17½ or 21 miles

These routes start from Thornhill Park and Ride, off the A40, east of Oxford. The 17½-mile ride explores the villages of the Oxford Heights and offers opportunities to see some of Oxfordshire's wonderful wildlife at the Otmoor RSPB reserve, Oakley Wood or Bernwood Meadows. Alternatively, you can enjoy Waterperry Gardens and church and the Rural Life Museum. The 7½-mile route takes riders to Wheatley, with its stone lock-up, and continues up to Shotover Country Park where a magnificent avenue of lime trees can be enjoyed, kites flown, picnics eaten and more wonders of the natural world explored on the many waymarked nature walks. If you are feeling energetic, the two can be combined into a 21-mile route.

Map: OS Landranger 164 Oxford, Chipping Norton and Bicester (GR SP566073).

Starting point: Thornhill Park and Ride (P&R) on the A40 just east of Oxford, where free parking is available. Alternatively for those with folding bikes, the P&R is served by the London and Gatwick/Heathrow coaches (X90, Oxford Tube & X70).

Refreshments: There is a café at Waterperry Gardens which is open 10 am to 5 pm in winter and to 5.30 pm in summer. It serves snacks and light lunches etc. Common Leys Farm also serves lunches and teas and coffee. For country pubs, we recommend the Abingdon Arms in Beckley or the Star at Stanton St John (just off the B4027).

The route: The 17½-mile route contains several short and sharp hills. There are several possible additions including a 2-mile detour to the Otmoor RSPB reserve, and a 1-mile detour to Waterperry Gardens. The 7½-mile route heads south and east to Shotover Country Park, and involves a single pull up to the park.

21- and 17½-mile routes

Exit the P&R, joining the path next to the exit road. **Bear L** parallel with the A40 (signed city centre). Soon cross the A40 using the underpass. **Bear R** and ride east (signed London/High Wycombe) along the A40 cycle track. (*)**Turn L** after 1 mile (signed Forest Hill) and climb Church Hill. **Turn L** at the T-junction with the B4027 (Stanton Road). There is a little-used tarmac path next to the road that you can use if you wish, as far as Stanton St John. On a good day you will enjoy views of the remnants of Bernwood Forest and Brill Hill in Buckinghamshire. Continue past the village. Soon you will see the polytunnels of Rectory Farm. A short detour down Pound Lane will take you to the farm shop and PYO.

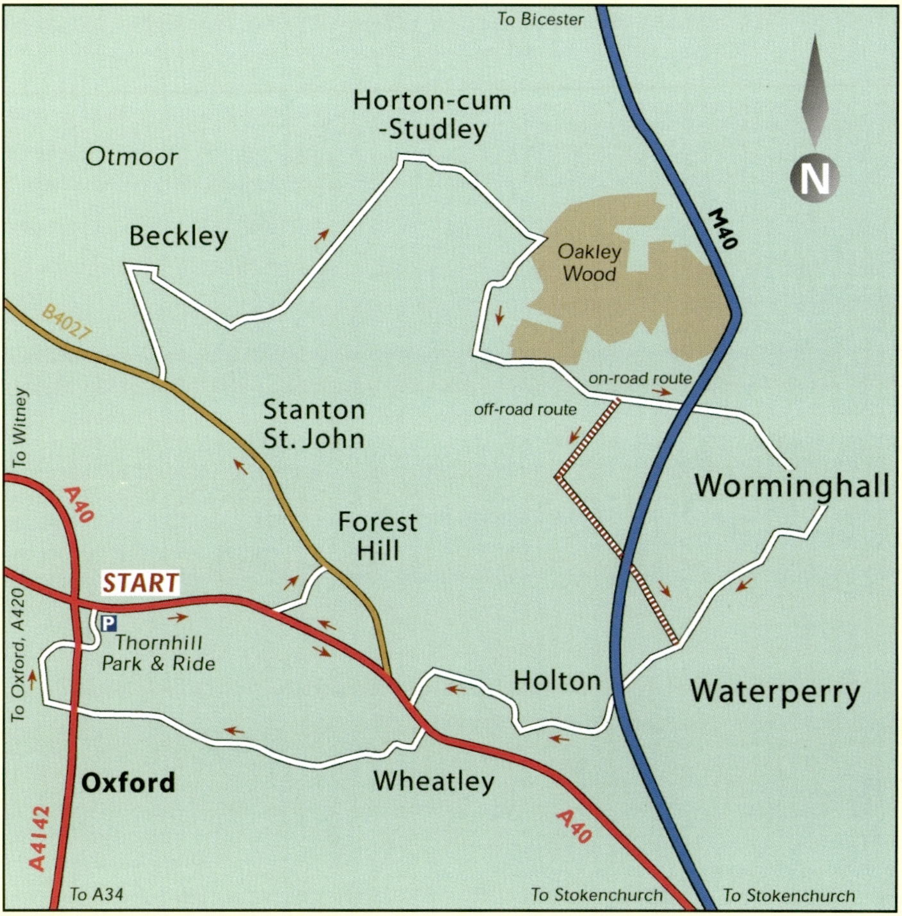

Map showing the route through Oxford Heights and Otmoor, with locations including Otmoor, Beckley, Horton-cum-Studley, Oakley Wood, Stanton St. John, Forest Hill, Worminghall, Waterperry, Holton, Wheatley, Oxford, and the START at Thornhill Park & Ride. Roads marked include B4027, A40, A420, A4142, M40. Directions: To Bicester, To Witney, To Oxford A420, To A34, To Stokenchurch. On-road route and off-road route are indicated.

Why not stop off to pick some soft fruit or, in season, asparagus for your tea? Check local press for opening hours.

Continue along the B4027 and take the second **turn R** along New Inn Road (signed Beckley, single track road). Ride into Beckley and **bear R** (take care, gravel on bend) onto High Street. Pass the Abingdon Arms pub on your left. If you would like to experience the magic of Otmoor first-hand, we recommend a 1 mile each way detour to the Otmoor RSPB reserve at the bottom of Otmoor

Lane. Even if you don't want to descend all the way down the hill, it's worth going a little way to enjoy views over the newly re-created wetland. When you are ready, ride out of Beckley up a short, steep hill (Roman Way) and onto Woodperry Road. **Turn L** at the T-junction (signed Horton-cum-Studley). Enjoy a long wooded descent.

In Horton-cum-Studley, **bear R** and climb Horton Hill. **Turn R** at the T-junction at the top of the hill (signed Stanton St John/Corner Farm). At the

13

Reedbeds at Otmoor

next T-junction you have arrived on the edge of Bernwood Forest. To your left, 100 yards up the road is the entrance to Oakley Wood. This is a good place for a picnic. The wood is well known for its butterflies, and has a waymarked butterfly trail. Otherwise, **turn R** and coast gently downhill. Soon, on your left, there is a small car park, the entrance to Bernwood Meadows, a nature reserve owned and managed by the Berks, Bucks and Oxon Wildlife Trust. In the first two weeks of May, you should be treated to a carpet of green-winged orchids, but there is plenty of wildlife interest all year. Continuing, **turn L** (signed Worminghall/Thame).

Soon you have a choice of a part off-road route over Waterperry Common

or an on-road route via Worminghall. If you opt for the Waterperry Common route, there is about 1 mile on a bridle track. This should only be undertaken in dry weather (unless you particularly like cleaning mud off your bike!). For the on-road route keep on, crossing the M40 and riding into Worminghall. **Turn R** at the crossroads in the village (Clifden Road) and follow this road for about 1½ miles. **Turn L** on a sharp right-hand bend for a detour to Waterperry Gardens (see below) or **bear R** (signed Waterperry Common) and meet the off-road route at (**).

For the off-road route, **turn R** along Smith's Lane (signed Commonleys Farm). After ½ mile, the road bends right to the farm (where a very good cream tea and other refreshments can

be had). Keep straight on, following bridle track signs. In particular, take care to **turn L** where the path forks at the interestingly-named Drunkards Bottom. After a while you should emerge and **turn L** onto tarmac at Parson's Farm. Cross the M40 and continue on to the T-junction. If you wish to visit Waterperry Gardens, **turn L** and **turn R** immediately on the bend (take care!). The gardens are through the village, ½ mile off the route. Otherwise **turn R** (signed Oxford/Wheatley) (**).

Re-cross the M40 and **turn R** (signed Holton). Ride through the village, bearing left (signed Oxford, Wheatley) and climbing the hill. If you want to return directly to Thornhill P&R (17½-mile route) look for a triangular cyclists crossing sign just past Wheatley Park School. Ahead and to your right is a path that takes you onto the A40 cycle track. Thornhill P&R is 2 miles along this track. Make sure to cross the A40 using the underpass.

For the 21-mile route, keep on the road (***). Cross over the A40 and enter Wheatley. Go straight over at the mini-roundabout onto Holloway Road. **Turn R** at the T-junction (signed Littleworth), passing the stone lock-up on your right. Keep straight ahead at the No Through Road sign and climb the hill. Near the top is a lodge house with wooden gates. Although not on the route, we can thoroughly recommend a short detour down the magnificent avenue of lime trees that used to greet visitors to Shotover House. In the spring, it's a lovely combination of fresh green leaves and bluebells. In autumn, enjoy the colours and the smell of decaying leaves. In high summer, it is a wonderful haven from the heat.

The main route continues onto the sandy track over Shotover Plain. To your left is Shotover Country Park with its many waymarked walks and a great place for flying kites and picnics. There is a cycle rack at the car park at the end of the sandy track if you wish to stop and tarry. When you are ready to continue, descend the hill with great care. Cross the ring road and **turn R** onto Quarry Road. **Turn R** at the crossroads (Quarry Hollow). Follow this road, **bearing L** then **R** onto Beaumont Road. **Turn R** by the Six Bells pub onto a road parallel to the ring road, and soon **turn L** onto a cycle track and cross the ring road at the pedestrian lights. **Turn R** onto Green Road and then Kiln Lane. **Turn L** at the crossroads (Downside Road) and **turn L** at the next crossroads (Collingwood Road). **Turn R** by the United Reformed church (London Road) and follow the road and then the track back to Thornhill P&R.

7½-mile route
Start off as for the other routes. At (*) keep straight on the cycle track for about 1 more mile. Approximately 200 yards after crossing the B4027 side turn, **bear L** and **turn R** onto the road (not signed). Continue on the main route at (***).

● ●

OTMOOR
Otmoor, or Otta's Moor, is a 4,000 acre expanse of fenland located 8 miles north-east of Oxford and ringed by seven villages, or as they are sometimes called 'Towns'. It is a haven for rare wildlife and much of the moor is now an area of special scientific interest (SSSI)

Riding down the lime avenue at Shotover

administered by the MOD who operate a rifle range on it. In 1997 the RSPB bought a large field in the centre of the moor and started the process of returning the moor to wet grazing pasture, primarily to provide good breeding conditions for wading birds such as lapwing, curlew, redshank and snipe which have been faring badly in the greater countryside. The Otmoor RSPB reserve now covers about 1,000 acres and supports some 90 pairs of breeding waders and numerous other birds and wildlife, including otters and rare brown and black hairstreak butterflies. The starling roost which, over the winter, regularly attracts up to 50,000 birds is one of nature's most amazing spectacles.

SHOTOVER

Shotover, located on the Oxford Heights east of Oxford, was originally part of a Royal Saxon hunting forest. However, heavy demand for oak for both fuel and fortification during the Civil War led to the removal of large parts of the woodland and subsequent opening up to grazing. Heathland developed on the sandy acidic soil. During the last century, woodland and scrub returned until a recent habitat restoration project began to restore some areas of heath. The result is that the Shotover Country Park is a rich and diverse area for wildlife, a mere 3 miles from the centre of Oxford, and much valued by residents and visitors alike. It is now criss-crossed by waymarked paths and offers stunning views from the car park at the top of the hill toward Oxford and the Chiltern Hills.

3

Woodstock: Green Lanes and Country Estates

29 or 12 miles, with alternative 19-mile route from Great Tew

This lovely route takes riders north out of Woodstock on the National Cycle Network Route 5, along an old 'green' lane before heading off to the picture-postcard village of Great Tew with its plethora of thatched cottages nestling at the bottom of a hill amid the parkland of the Great Tew Estate. The route then goes east along a limestone ridge overlooking the valley of the River Swere, before heading south along the Cherwell Valley and back to Woodstock, passing Rousham House and gardens. The route is undulating, but never hilly and takes in many pleasant villages and some beautiful scenery. It is also possible to ride a shorter 12-mile route from Woodstock. Alternatively, the entire ride, or a shorter 19-mile loop may be ridden starting and finishing at Great Tew.

Map: OS Landranger 164 Oxford, Chipping Norton and Bicester (GR SP444167).

Starting points: The main route starts and finishes outside the church on Park Street, Woodstock (10 miles north-west of Oxford on the A44). There is a free car park on Hensington Road (east of the A44). If you park here, you can access the route simply by turning left out of the car park. For riders with folding bikes, there is a regular bus service from Oxford (Stagecoach, route S3). Alternatively, the ride can be ridden starting and finishing at Great Tew. There is a free car park in the village (GR SP395294). The main route and 12-mile route can also be readily accessed from Tackley railway station (Oxford to Banbury line). The main route and 19-mile route can be easily accessed from Heyford railway station (also on the Oxford to Banbury line). Both railway stations are less than ½ mile from the routes.

Refreshments: Woodstock itself has plenty of restaurants, cafés and pubs to suit all tastes. There is also a café at the Oxfordshire Museum, opposite the church. At Great Tew, we recommend the Faulkland Arms. There are also pubs serving food at Duns Tew (the White Horse Inn) and Steeple Aston (the White Lion). Tackley village shop (located in the village hall) can provide sandwiches and drinks.

The route: The main route proceeds north from Woodstock using Dornford Lane (an old green lane) before continuing on-road into countryside typical of the limestone uplands of north Oxfordshire; there is a steep hill at Steeple Aston.

Riding through North Aston

The 29-mile route

With your back to the church, **turn R** along Park Street and **bear R** by the town hall. Go straight over at the crossroads with the A44 (use the nearby pedestrian lights if this proves difficult) and ride down Hensington Road. **Turn L** down Green Lane and descend the hill. **Turn R** at the bottom (signed Banbury/NCN Route 5). **Turn L** onto a wooded track and continue to the road. Go through a gate and cross the road. Continue riding along the track for just under 2 miles and then go straight ahead joining a single track road. **Turn L** at the T-junction (signed Banbury/NCN Route 5) (*).

Turn R (signed Glympton/Banbury/ NCN Route 5). **Turn R** at the crossroads (signed Barton/Sandford). Go straight ahead at the next crossroads (parting company with NCN 5) and also go straight ahead at the crossroads with the B4030 (signed Sandford/Ledwell/ Worton). **Turn L** into Sandford St Martin (signed Sandford/Great Tew/Barford) and ride through the village, **bearing R** by the cross and passing the church on your right. **Turn L** at the crossroads (signed Great & Little Tew/Chipping Norton). Soon you will notice the parkland associated with the Great Tew Estate on your right and its magnificent trees (mainly oaks and limes). **Turn R** and descend the hill into Great Tew village. The car park is at the bottom of the hill on the right, just beyond the village green with its shop and inn.

(***) When you are ready to continue, retrace by climbing the hill and **turning L** at the junction at the top (signed Duns Tew/Ledwell). **Turn L** at the crossroads (signed Nether

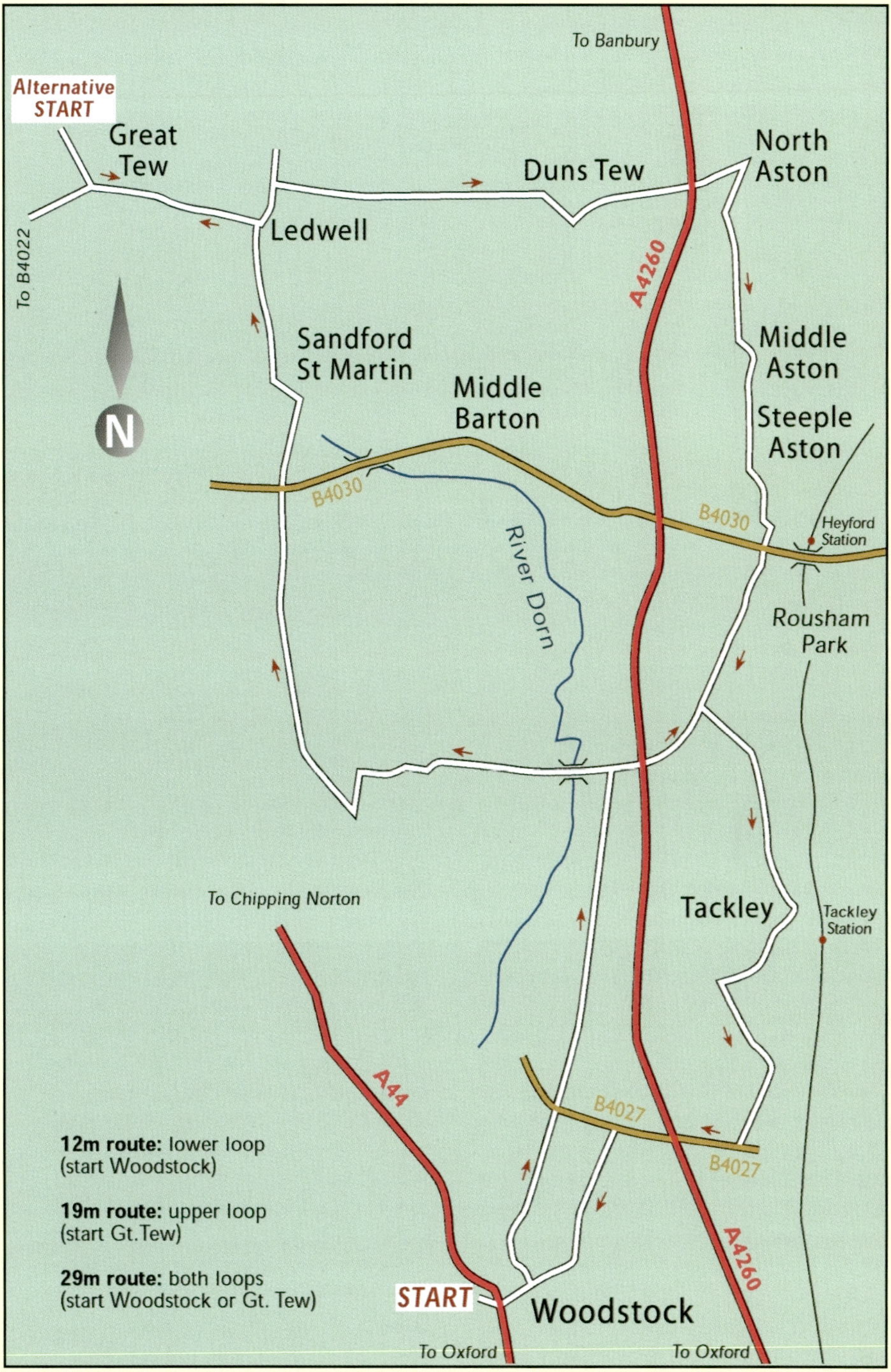

Alternative
START

Great
Tew

To B4022

Ledwell

Duns Tew

North
Aston

A4260

To Banbury

Sandford
St Martin

Middle
Aston

Steeple
Aston

Middle
Barton

B4030

B4030

Heyford
Station

River Dorn

Rousham
Park

To Chipping Norton

Tackley

Tackley
Station

A44

B4027

B4027

A4260

12m route: lower loop
(start Woodstock)

19m route: upper loop
(start Gt. Tew)

29m route: both loops
(start Woodstock or Gt. Tew)

START

Woodstock

To Oxford

To Oxford

N

Sandford St Martin

Worton/Barford/Duns Tew) and descend the hill carefully. Soon **turn R** (signed Duns Tew). Ride through Duns Tew following signs to North Aston. Carefully go straight over at the crossroads with the A4260 (signed North Aston/Somerton). **Turn R** on the outskirts of North Aston (signed Middle Aston) and **turn L** at the T-junction (signed Middle Aston House). Ahead and to your left, look out for the water towers and other buildings of Upper Heyford airbase, once home to nuclear weapons, the USAF and one of the first women's peace camps. These days all that is gone, but moves are afoot to preserve some of it as a permanent reminder of the Cold War, including a nuclear bunker.

Ride into Steeple Aston and descend the steep hill and climb the other side (aptly named Paine's Hill!). **Turn L** by the village shop (not signed). Ride out of the village, descending the steep hill (CARE!). Go straight over at the traffic lights (signed Rousham). The entrance to Rousham Park is ahead and on your left. **Turn L** (signed Nethercott/Tackley) (**). Follow the main road through Tackley and climb the hill passing the church. **Turn L** (signed Whitehill). **Turn R** at the T-junction at Bunkers Hill and proceed to a staggered crossroads with the A4260. Cross carefully (signed Wootton/Glympton). **Turn L** at the crossroads (signed Hensington/Woodstock). **Turn R** at the mini-roundabout on the edge of Woodstock (signed 'Town Centre'). The car park is soon on your right. To return to the church, continue and go straight over the crossroads with the A44. **Bear left** onto Park Street. The church is soon on your left.

12-mile route
Follow the main route as far as the junction marked (*). **Turn R** (signed Tackley). **Turn L** onto the A4260 (signed Deddington) and immediately **turn R**, with care, (signed Rousham, CARE!). Rejoin the main route at the junction marked (**) and **turn R** (signed Nethercott/Tackley).

19-mile route from Great Tew
Follow the main route from Great Tew (***) to the junction just beyond Rousham (**). Go straight ahead (signed Wootton) and **turn L** onto the A4260 (signed Kidlington) and immediately **turn R**, with care (signed Wootton), rejoining the main route at the junction marked (*).

● ●

WOODSTOCK AND BLENHEIM PALACE
Woodstock was a royal manor before the Norman Conquest and so the town and its adjoining park have ancient royal roots. Henry I enclosed the park for hunting and Henry II enlarged the original palace and built 'New Woodstock' to house his court. The medieval palace continued to be used by succeeding monarchs, but was destroyed beyond repair during the Civil War. In 1704, the manor and park were given to the first Duke of Marlborough by Queen Anne, in gratitude for his victory at Blenheim. The house was designed by Vanbrugh and built over the period 1705–1722. The 2,500 acre estate was landscaped by Capability Brown about 50 years later. The River Glyme is used to feed several magnificent lakes. The house contains many interesting treasures including carvings by Grinling Gibbons and an amazing series of Belgian tapestries depicting scenes from the battle of Blenheim. The house is open

from March through to October, and the grounds are open all year. An entrance fee is charged for both. Woodstock is also home to the Oxfordshire County Museum which houses permanent displays on the history and life of the county. Its latest attraction is a dinosaur garden featuring both a life size model of a megalosaurus, whose bones were first found in Oxfordshire and described by William Buckland in 1824, and casts of a 168 million year old dinosaur trackway unearthed in Ardley near Bicester. Entrance is free and the museum is open 10 am to 5 pm Tuesday to Saturday and 2 pm to 5 pm on Sundays.

ROUSHAM PARK
Rousham House was built in 1635 by Sir Robert Dormer and is still in the ownership of the same family. William Kent added the wings and a stable block around 1738. The house was extensively redecorated in the 18th century, although significant features from the earlier Jacobean house remain. From a historical perspective, the most important feature of the park is its landscape gardens which descend gently to the banks of the River Cherwell. They are probably the earliest unaltered example of English landscape design and also one of the best preserved works of William Kent. The garden was set out as a series of terraces with fountains, cascades, statues and buildings in the Italian taste. The views are skilfully manipulated by the use of hedges and trees to provide what seems like a series of garden tableaux. The house is open on Wednesdays and Sundays (and Bank Holiday Mondays) 2 pm to 4.30 pm April to September. The gardens are open daily 10 am to 4.30 pm. No children under 15 or dogs.

21

4

Charlbury and the Royal Hunting Forest of Wychwood

9½, 12½ or 17 miles

Leaving Charlbury, this route crosses the River Evenlode before climbing gently out of the Evenlode valley. It then joins a wonderful road through some of the fragmented remains of the royal hunting forest of Wychwood. The road rises and falls for some 2 miles before a swooping descent to what is locally known as Five Ash Bottom. A short climb to the village of Leafield follows. From here the route descends gradually to meet the B4022. At this point there is a choice. The main route continues through the villages of Ramsden and New Yatt before a gentle climb to North Leigh. Soon after, the route meets the River Evenlode again and from then on, it is never far away as we return to Charlbury. Two shorter routes can also be chosen.

Map: OS Landranger 164 Oxford, Chipping Norton and Bicester (GR SP357195).

Starting point: All three routes start and finish in the centre of the small town of Charlbury, where Church Street, Market Street, Sheep Street and Browns Lane all meet (15 miles north-west of Oxford). If you arrive by car, there is a free car park at the Spendlove Centre on Enstone Road (B4022). Alternatively, Charlbury is located on the London to Worcester (via Oxford) railway line. If you want to travel by train, take care to get into one of the correct carriages because there is a short platform at Charlbury station! To join the route from there, simply ride out of the station and turn L at the T-junction.

Refreshments: There are several pubs in Charlbury itself. We recommend the Bull, which is located in the centre on the corner of Sheep Street and Brown's Lane. Along the route there are pubs serving food at Leafield, Ramsden and Finstock. The Ramsden Garden Centre, located about ½ mile off the route just off the B4022 south-west of Finstock, has a café where meals, snacks and other light refreshments are sold. If you prefer your refreshments al fresco, then why not find a shaded spot in Wychwood or by the Roman villa near North Leigh? However, if rivers are your thing, then turn L on entering Fawler (by Manor Farm); this takes you down to a pleasant village green with a seat and straight ahead there is a footpath down to the River Evenlode. It's a quiet spot and you can sit on the wooden bridge and dangle your legs and watch the river flowing below you.

The route: There are several climbs, but also several descents to enjoy along the way. None of the climbs are too steep, though, and so one or other of the options can be tackled by all the family.

Ramsden village centre

17-mile route

Head off in a northerly direction (Market Street, signed Burford/ Chipping Norton). **Turn L** (signed Burford B4437). After a short descent the road crosses the River Evenlode and a short distance further along passes by the railway station on the left. Then there is a steady climb offering views across the Evenlode valley. After about a mile, and near the top of the climb, **turn L** (signed Leafield). This road meanders through some of the remains of the once royal hunting forest of Wychwood. Look out for wildlife such as foxes and deer. Continue on into Leafield. **Turn L** at the T-junction (signed Finstock/Charlbury). Continue on to the junction with the B4022 (*).

Go straight over (CARE) (High Street, not signed). Soon **turn R** (signed Mount Skippett). Now you can boast about riding down a mountain! **Turn L** at the T-junction (not signed), then ride through Ramsden. Go straight over at a staggered crossroads (signed North Leigh/Witney). Also go straight over at the next crossroads (signed North Leigh/Witney).

Turn L (signed New Yatt/Northleigh). Ride into New Yatt, then **turn L** at the T-junction (signed North Leigh). Ride into North Leigh and **turn L** into Church Road (not signed). Descend, passing the church on your left, to the T-junction and **turn R** (signed Hanborough/Witney). **Turn L** (signed East End) and ride through East End. At the far side of the village there is a bridlepath (rough going) on the right leading down to the Roman villa should you wish to visit.

Shortly after, there is a steep descent

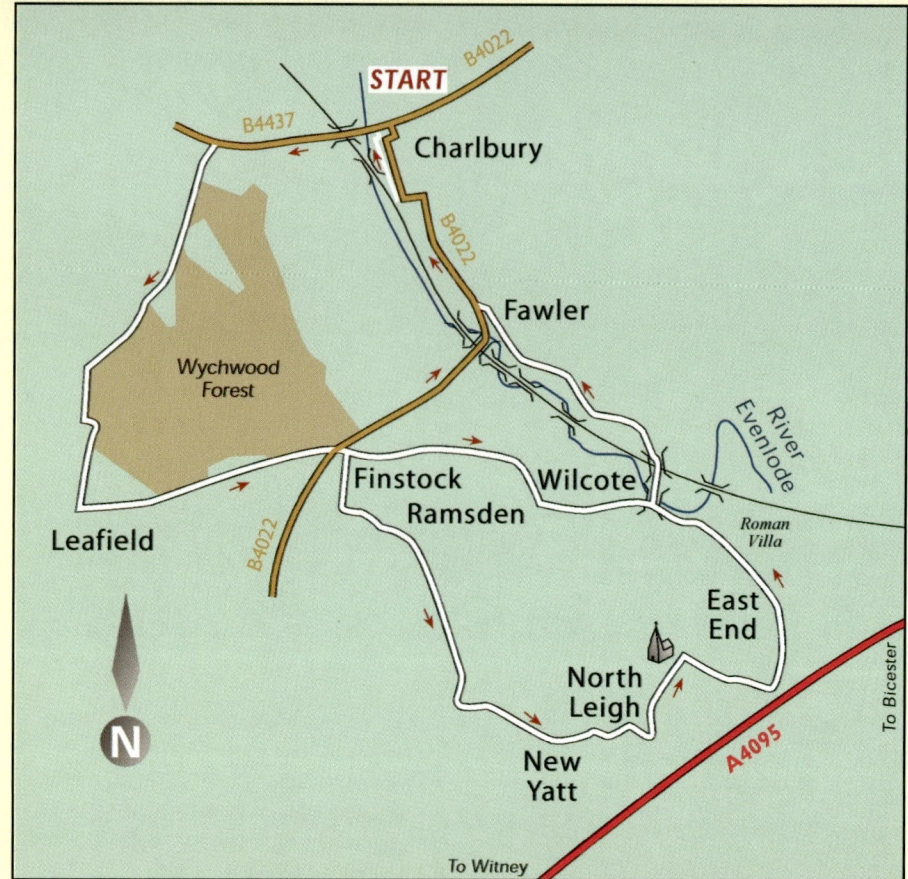

with a crossroads at the bottom. **Turn R** here (signed Stonesfield/Woodstock). (**) Climb to the next junction and cross the railway line. **Turn L** (signed Fawler/Charlbury). **Turn L** at the T-junction (not signed) and ride through Fawler. **Turn R** at the T-junction with the B4022 (signed Charlbury/Enstone) (***) and ride into the edge of Charlbury. At the T-junction (Woodstock Road), **turn L** and immediately **turn L** again following signs for Cornbury Park and the town centre. Enjoy a gentle sweeping descent with Cornbury Park and House on your left. This road eventually becomes Church Street which takes you back to the crossroads at the start of the ride.

12½-mile route
Follow the 17-mile route as far as (*). Go straight over (CARE!) onto High Street, Finstock (not signed). Take care on the descent along the length of High Street. At the end of the descent the street name appropriately becomes 'The Bottom'! Keep straight ahead (signed Wilcote). There is a short sharp climb so be prepared! **Turn L** at the crossroads at the edge of Wilcote (signed East End/Stonesfield). The road

24

Charlbury

descends to another crossroads and the last bit is steep, so take care. **Turn L** (signed Stonesfield/Woodstock). Rejoin the 17 mile route at (**).

9½-mile route
Follow the 17-mile route as far as (*). **Turn L** here (signed Charlbury/ Chipping Norton) and follow the B4022 into the edge of Charlbury. Rejoin the 17-mile route at (***).

CHARLBURY
The town of Charlbury lies in the valley of the River Evenlode, one of the Thames' many tributaries. Today it is a quiet place of pleasant stone cottages and handsome old inns. Not far from the town lies the large estate of Cornbury Park and also the remains of the once great hunting forest of Wychwood. For many centuries Charlbury was well known for its glove manufacture, an industry which at its height employed more than 1,000 people. Apparently, in Chalbury's heyday, there were more than 20 pubs; a fact which set us wondering how many of Charlbury's gloves had other than the usual number of fingers! For those interested in country crafts, Charlbury has a small museum which preserves many facets of rural life and is open on Sunday afternoons from Easter to October.

WYCHWOOD FOREST
Wychwood Forest was once a great royal hunting forest that covered most of what is now West Oxfordshire. Even in Norman times, the boundaries of the forest were defined by the two rivers, Windrush and Glyme. In those days the term 'forest' referred to an area which was under the jurisdiction of Forest Law, i.e. laws defining who could use the resources of the forest. The 'forest' would therefore also have included meadows, cultivated fields, heaths and downs, in addition to woodlands. The name Wychwood is believed to come from the name of the Saxon tribe Hwicce who once occupied the area. It was in the reign of Ethelred II (978–1016) that the royal hunting forest was established and a hunting lodge built at Woodstock. In 1864, the ten square miles remaining in the royal forest were taken out of Forest Law by a parliamentary law of disafforestation and local residents compensated. This rapidly led to conversion of much of the remaining woodland to farmland. Nowadays only 870 hectares of woodland remain but it is well protected as a National Nature Reserve and SSSI.

Chipping Norton: In Search of the Father of Modern Geology

7, 11½ or 22 miles

These routes start and finish in the small town of Chipping Norton. The full route leaves the town to the south-west and visits the village of Churchill, with its church tower a scaled-down version of Magdalen Tower in Oxford. There are various memorials and fountains on the village green and the village has associations with William Smith, the father of modern geology. The route continues through Kingham to explore the villages of Milton and Ascott under Wychwood before returning through Chadlington. The 11½-mile route cuts through directly from Churchill to Chadlington before rejoining the longer route. On this route you will pass the ancient earthworks of Knollbury. The 7-mile route also leaves to the south-west before heading east and climbing to get fantastic views back to the town and the Bliss Tweed Mill.

Maps: OS Landranger 164 Oxford, Chipping Norton and Bicester and 163 Cheltenham and Cirencester (GR SP313270).

Starting point: Outside the Fox Hotel in the Market Place, Chipping Norton (some 20 miles north-west of Oxford on the A44. There is a free car park located just off the A44 (Worcester Road) to the western side of the town. There is no railway station. The nearest station is 7 miles away at Charlbury on the Cotswold Line between Oxford and Worcester.

Refreshments: There is a choice of pubs and cafés in Chipping Norton itself. Just south of the route there is a good choice of pubs in Shipton-under-Wychwood (the Shaven Crown, the Lamb or the Red Horse). The Tite Inn at Chadlington is also a good option. If you want to picnic, then the village green at Churchill is very pleasant (if a bit close to the start). Alternatively there is a path more or less opposite the Tite Inn which is pleasant to follow and you can picnic next to the Chadlington Brook.

The route: All three routes involve climbing, after all this is the Cotswolds! However, don't be put off, they can all be taken steadily and offer marvellous views of open countryside and some heady descents as incentives.

22-mile route

Starting outside the Fox Hotel (on the left) follow the sign, outside the hotel, for Churchill and Bledington. Go straight ahead at the mini-roundabout (signed Churchill/Charlbury/Burford B4450). Leave Chipping Norton behind you, and after 1 mile keep straight ahead at the staggered crossroads and ride into Churchill. (*)

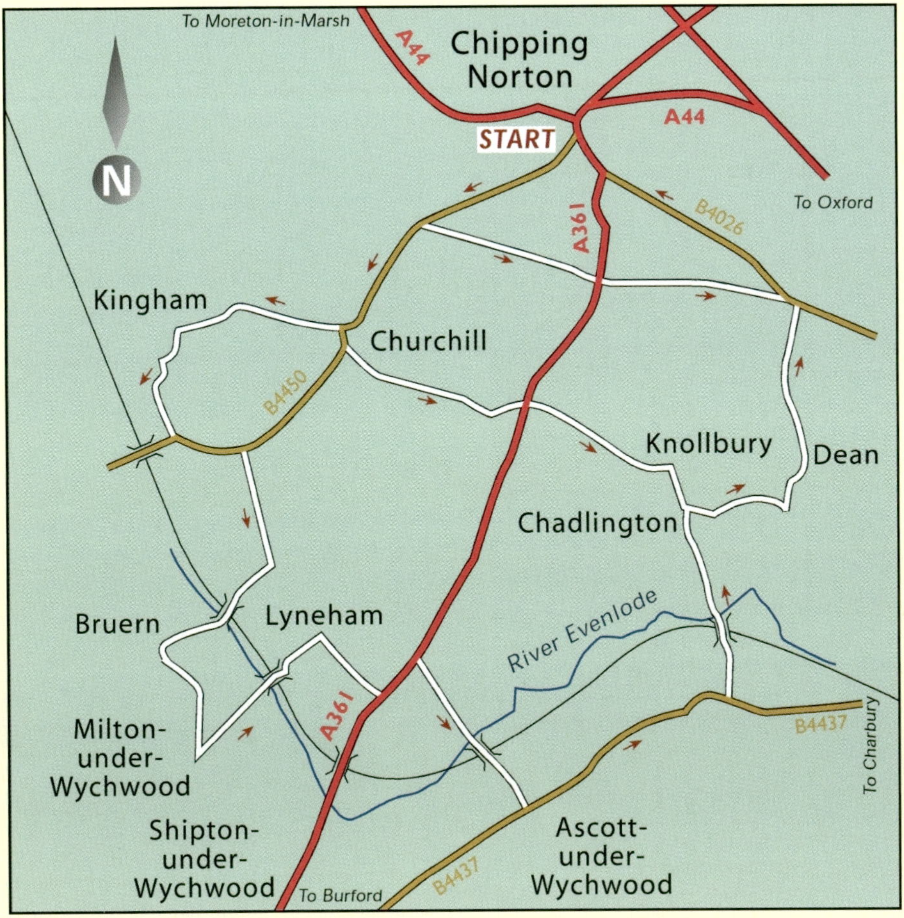

Turn R in Churchill into Kingham Road (signed Kingham). Ride into Kingham and **turn L** at the crossroads (signed Kingham Station; note: signpost obscured by tree). Ride out of the village then **turn L** at the T-junction (signed Churchill/Chipping Norton). **Turn R** (signed Lyneham/ Shipton). **Turn R** (signed Bruern/ Milton under Wychwood). Take care at the level crossing and ride through Bruern.

Turn L (signed Milton under Wychwood/Shipton under Wychwood) and **turn L** on the edge of Milton under Wychwood (signed Lyneham). Ride into Lyneham and keep straight ahead until you reach the T-junction at the far end of the village. **Turn R** (signed Shipton under Wychwood). **Turn L** at the top of a steady climb (signed Banbury/Chipping Norton A361). Soon **turn R** (signed Ascott under Wychwood). Descend into the village. In Ascott under Wychwood take care at the level crossing and **bear L** (signed Leafield). **Turn L** at the top of

The memorial fountain in Churchill

the steady climb (signed Charlbury, B4437).

Ride along the B4437 for approximately 2 miles and enjoy the views of the Evenlode valley to your left. **Turn L** at the crossroads (signed Chadlington/Chipping Norton). Ride into Chadlington and **turn R** at the staggered crossroads (signed Dean/Spelsbury).

(**) **Turn L** (signed Dean) – please note, this turning is slightly hidden by the curve in the road. Ride through the tiny hamlet of Dean, keeping straight on at the junction with a tree on a grass triangle, and continue to climb until reaching the T-junction. **Turn L** (not signed) and proceed to the T-junction with the A361. (***) **Turn R** onto Burford Road on the edge of Chipping Norton and descend the hill

with a school on your right. **Turn L** at the mini-roundabout (signed Town Centre/Through Traffic), then **turn R** at the second mini-roundabout (signed Banbury/Oxford/Evesham).

11½-mile route
Follow the 22 mile route as far as Churchill (*). Ride through the village and **bear L** by the church (signed Sarsden/Merriscourt). Keep straight ahead until the T-junction at the top of the climb. **Turn L** (signed Banbury/Chipping Norton A361). Immediately **turn R** (signed Chadlington). About halfway down the hill, on the left, is an ancient earthwork called Knollbury. Care is needed entering Chadlington, as the road is rather narrow. **Turn R** at the T-junction (signpost damaged) and keep straight ahead until arriving at a staggered crossroads. **Turn L** (signed

Dean/Spelsbury). Follow the 22-mile route from (**).

7-mile route
Start off following the 22-mile route, but **turn L** at the staggered crossroads about 1 mile outside Chipping Norton (signed Lidstone). There is now a steady climb. Take a look to your left. On this loop we get the best view of the famous Bliss Tweed Mill building, now turned into apartments. There is also a good view back to Chipping Norton itself. Go straight ahead at the crossroads with the A361 (signed Lidstone). **Turn L** onto the B4026 at the next T-junction (not signed) and start heading back to Chipping Norton, rejoining the 22-mile route at (***).

● ●

CHURCHILL
Churchill is a small village on high ground a few miles south-west of Chipping Norton. It boasts two famous sons, Warren Hastings (first governor of India) and William Smith (the father of modern geology). You can find out more about them and other aspects of Churchill's long history at the Churchill Heritage Centre, which is located in the chancel of the old medieval church and is open on Saturday and Sunday afternoons (April to September) from 2 pm to 4.30 pm. Entrance is free. Churchill has a large village green with several

monuments, including a memorial fountain erected in 1870 in memory of James Langston. The architectural historian Nikolaus Pevsner describes it as 'memorably ugly'; see what you think.

WILLIAM SMITH
William Smith was born in Churchill in 1769, the son of a blacksmith and the eldest of five children. Early on in life he developed an interest in geometry and drawing and when he was 18 he became apprentice to a surveyor in nearby Stow on the Wold. At the end of the 18th century surveyors were in increasing demand, especially with the boom in canal building. It was a profession that someone from the working classes, like Smith, could aspire to. Eventually he started his own business. The combination of surveying skills and an interest in fossils led him to the realisation that sedimentary rocks could be identified by the assemblage of fossils they contained and furthermore that outcrops of specific rock types occurred all over the country and always in the same order or stratigraphy. This information, gleaned during his many surveying trips was eventually published as the first recognisably modern geological map with different rock types indicated using colour. The memorial to William Smith in Churchill was erected in 1891 and is suitably constructed from a monolith of local stone.

6
Hitting the Heights from Chipping Norton

27 miles

From Chipping Norton this route heads onto the open roads with wide views of the limestone uplands, visiting Enstone and the Hoar Stone, the remains of a prehistoric burial mound, before continuing on narrow winding roads to the pleasant village of Sandford St Martin with its preaching cross, manor house and mellow stone cottages. The route then takes you north and westwards into more open, hilly country, visiting the large village of Hook Norton where you can visit a small local pottery and a steam-powered brewery. Don't be too tempted to sample the produce though, because you still have some steep hills ahead of you as you ride through Great Rollright, past the famous prehistoric Rollright Stones and back into Chipping Norton via Over Norton.

Maps: OS Landranger 164 Oxford, Chipping Norton and Bicester and 151 Stratford-upon-Avon, Warwick and Banbury (GR SP313270).

Starting point: The Fox Hotel in the Market Place, Chipping Norton (some 20 miles north-west of Oxford on the A44. There is a free car park located just off the A44 (Worcester Road) to the western side of the town. There is no railway station; the nearest station is 7 miles away at Charlbury on the Cotswold line between Oxford and Worcester.

Refreshments: There is a good choice of pubs and cafés in Chipping Norton Itself. There aren't too many pubs along the route. However, Hook Norton provides a welcome oasis and the Pear Tree pub is well worth a visit. You will also find plenty of nice spots along the way to rest and enjoy the view or have a picnic.

The route: This route takes riders on an exhilarating trip around the sometimes hilly countryside of north Oxfordshire. In short, this is a route for the more experienced cyclist who doesn't mind a few gradients to spice up a ride!

Outside the Fox Hotel, start by following the road signed to Churchill B4450/Burford A361. **Turn L** at the mini-roundabout (signed Burford/ Charlbury A361) and **turn R** at a second mini-roundabout (signed Burford A361). Climb out of the town and **turn L** (signed Charlbury/ Spelsbury B4026). After a further gentle climb, **turn L** (signed Lidstone/ Enstone) and follow this road into Enstone. **Turn R** at the T-junction (not signed). The Hoar Stone, the remains of a prehistoric burial mound, is located

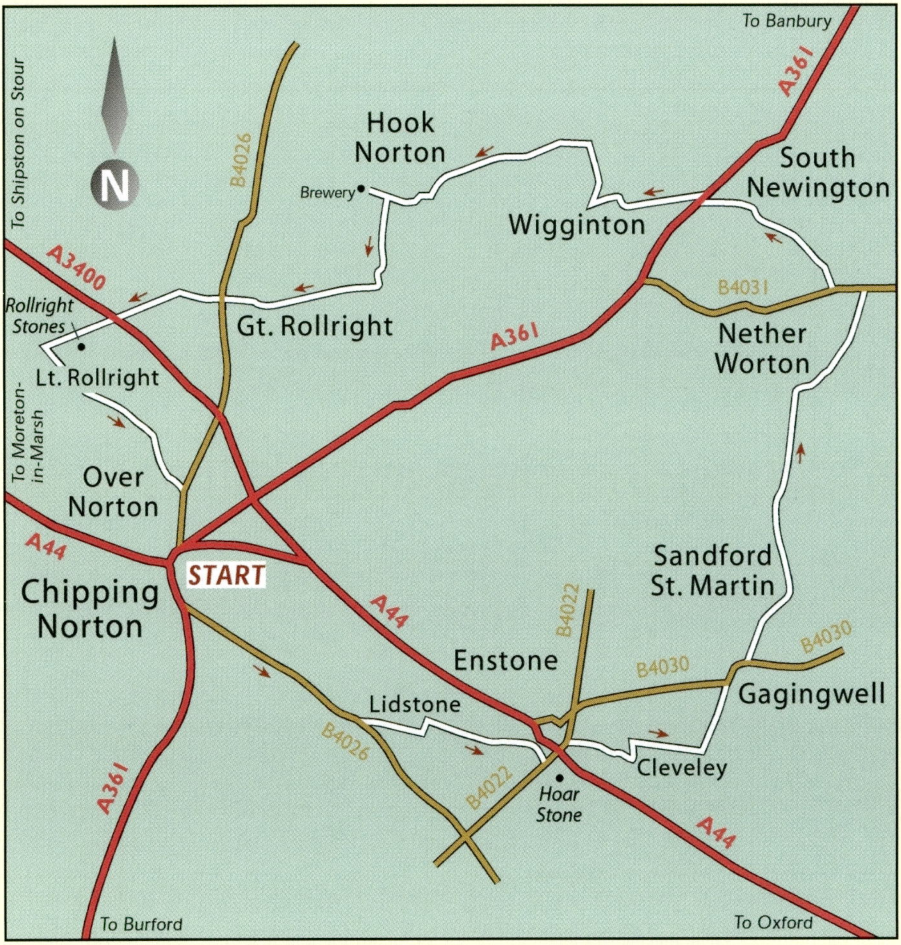

To Banbury

A361

To Shipston on Stour

B4026

Hook Norton

Brewery●

Wigginton

South Newington

N

A3400

B4031

Rollright Stones

Gt. Rollright

A361

Nether Worton

Lt. Rollright

To Moreton-in-Marsh

Over Norton

A44

START

Chipping Norton

A361

A44

Sandford St. Martin

B4022

B4030

B4030

Enstone

B4030

Gagingwell

Lidstone

B4026

B4022

●Hoar Stone

Cleveley

A44

To Burford

To Oxford

opposite the following junction. To visit it, go straight ahead at the crossroads and the stone is immediately on your right. Otherwise **turn L** (signed B4022/Enstone/Great Tew) and descend to the A44. Go straight across at the staggered crossroads (signed The Tews/Bicester). Take care descending as it is soon necessary to **turn R** along the single track road (signed Cleveley).

Ride into Cleveley and **turn L** (signed Radford). The road climbs steeply out of the village, so it is a good idea to get into a low gear in readiness before the turn. Take care on all these narrow roads as gravel gets washed onto them after rain and can make cornering dangerous. **Turn L** at the crossroads (signed Gagingwell). In Gagingwell, **turn R** at the T-junction (not signed) and after a short climb and on a right-hand bend, **turn L** (signed Sandford).

Ride into Sandford St Martin, and **turn L** at the green triangle with a preaching cross and large yew tree (not signed). Pass the church and ride out of the

Chipping Norton's handsome town hall

village. Keep straight ahead following signs to Nether Worton. **Turn L** in the centre of the village to join NCN route 5 (signed Barford/Bloxham). Climb to the crossroads with the B4031. **Turn L** onto the B4031 (signed Chipping Norton) and soon carefully **turn R** (signed South Newington). Stay on this road until the T-junction with the A361. **Turn R** (signed Banbury) and shortly **turn L** (signed Wigginton). Ride into the village and soon **turn L** (not signed). Pass the village hall on your left. Keep straight ahead to a T-junction. **Turn R** (signed Hook Norton/Tadmarton). **Turn L** at the crossroads and ride into Hook Norton.

Enter Hook Norton along Station Road and soon ride into East End. If you wish to visit the pottery, you will soon see it on your left. Continue down Chapel Lane and **bear L** (signed Chipping Norton). Follow the road through the village, passing the church on the right. After a steep and narrow descent, **turn R** (signed The Firs) then almost immediately **turn L** down Brewery Lane and take a look at Hook Norton Brewery which is sometimes open for tours, has its own shop, and is still powered by a steam engine. When you are ready (and assuming you are still able!) retrace your steps and **turn R** by the Pear Tree pub (signed Great Rollright/Chipping Norton) and start climbing out of the village. Stay on this road, following signs for Great Rollright, and ride into the village. Keep straight ahead at the crossroads (signed Long Compton/Little Rollright) and **turn L** at a T-junction (signed Little Rollright). Continue till you arrive at the staggered crossroads with the A3400. Go straight over (signed Little Rollright/Long Compton). Soon

The Hoar Stone

hill, between the church and the brook. Here, in around 1120, a sizeable motte and bailey castle was built. Now all that remains are some earthworks, and Pool Meadow, once a medieval fishpond. In 1205 it was decided to build a new market place, in its present position at the top of the hill, to help promote trade. King John granted a charter to hold a fair which made the town wealthy because they could charge tolls to trade. Soon the citizens were building magnificent houses, paying to improve the church, building almshouses and a school. Today many of these buildings remain, although sometimes they have been altered according to the fashion. In the 19th century, Chipping Norton's economy was dominated by the Bliss Tweed Mill, brewing and glove-making. Nowadays it is the centre of a thriving local antiques trade.

you will come across the prehistoric Rollright Stones on your left.

To complete the ride, continue to the next crossroads and **turn L** (signed Little Rollright). Keep straight ahead down the steep descent, then climb out of the valley and near the top **turn R** (signed Over Norton) and ride into the village. **Turn R** at the T-junction in the village (signed Chipping Norton). On entering Chipping Norton, there is a double mini-roundabout. Follow the signs for Evesham A44/Burford A361/Town Centre. Care is needed on this sometimes busy junction. Keep straight ahead until reaching the Fox Hotel and the end of the ride.

● ● ● ● ● ● ● ● ● ● ● ● ● ● ● ● ● ● ●

CHIPPING NORTON
In Norman times, Norton, as it was then known, was located at the bottom of the

THE ROLLRIGHT STONES
The Rollright Stones consist of three main features, located within 200 yards of each other on a ridge between Over Norton and Long Compton. Tradition has it that they represent a king, some of his treacherous knights and men who were turned to stone during a confrontation with a witch. In reality, however, the stone circle, the King's Stone and the Whispering Knights date from different periods and their close proximity seems to be due to our ancestors' penchant for reusing old sacred sites. Indeed, there are also less obvious Roman and Saxon features close by, so the trend continued. The oldest of the three is the Whispering Knights, believed to be a Portal Dolmen' burial chamber, in use from 3800–3000 BC. The stone circle itself (the most easterly in the country) originally consisted of 105 stones (all local to the site) which formed a continuous ring with a single entrance.

The King's Stone

The circle is big enough to hold 200 people; although we have no knowledge of what (if any) ceremonies took place there. Finally, the King's Stone is believed to have marked a Bronze Age burial site.

HOOK NORTON BREWERY
Hook Norton Brewery was founded by a local farmer and maltster, John Harris, in 1849 and is now one of only 32 independent family-run breweries in the country. It is a fine example of a Victorian tower brewery, and the Brewery Centre (and shop) is open from Monday to Saturday, 9.30 am to 4.30 pm and there are regular tours, which are fascinating. It is often possible to watch the brewing process in action, especially if you take a morning tour. They last approximately two hours. History is very important to the business and there is also a small museum on the site showing aspects of rural life. In 1985 the brewery began once again to deliver to local pubs using a dray drawn by shire horses.

Burford: Gateway to the Cotswolds

9, 18 or 26 miles

The longest of these three routes starts by visiting Filkins with its small rural museum and Cotswold Woollen Weavers, then continues to Langford with its Saxon church. There is the possibility of a short detour to visit Kelmscott, a village ever associated with William Morris and the Arts and Crafts movement. The return is through Clanfield, Broadwell and Kencot before climbing gently back into Cotswold scenery at Shilton. Why not stop and have a break by the ford or a pint at the village pub? All that is left to do is to cross the A40 and enjoy the descent into the Windrush valley and Swinbrook before heading back, guided by the sight of the spire of Burford church. The middle ride cuts straight across from Filkins to Broadwell, and the short ride passes the Cotswold Wildlife Park, a good place for a family day out.

Map: OS Landranger 163 Cheltenham and Cirencester (GR SP253124).

Starting point: This ride starts from the parish church in Burford, located just east of the High Street. It is an impressive landmark and can be seen for miles around. It is a short distance from the free car park, located at the lower end of Burford. This is accessed from the main street by following the parking signs into Church Lane. Burford is a popular destination, and the car park may get full at busy times.

Refreshments: Burford contains a wide variety of pubs, restaurants, hotels and tea rooms. We recommend the Priory Tearooms on High Street and the Royal Oak on Witney Street. There is a tea room at Cotswold Woollen Weavers at Filkins and there is a restaurant serving teas, coffees and light lunches at Kelmscott Manor during opening hours. There are also pubs along the route at Langford and Shilton. For those riding the 9-mile loop, refreshments are also available for visitors to the Cotswold Wildlife Park.

The route: This ride offers plenty of choice and the possibility to cut it short should you feel tired or simply spend more time than you expected exploring the various attractions along the way. The route begins along the flat roads of the Thames floodplain, with a gentle ascent at Shilton and an exhilarating descent back into the Windrush valley.

26-mile route

With your back to the church, **turn R**. **Turn L** at the T-junction (High Street) and immediately **turn R** into Priory Lane (CARE!). Go straight ahead at the staggered crossroads into Tanners Lane. **Turn R** at the T-junction with the A40 (not signed), soon **turn L** (signed

Burford

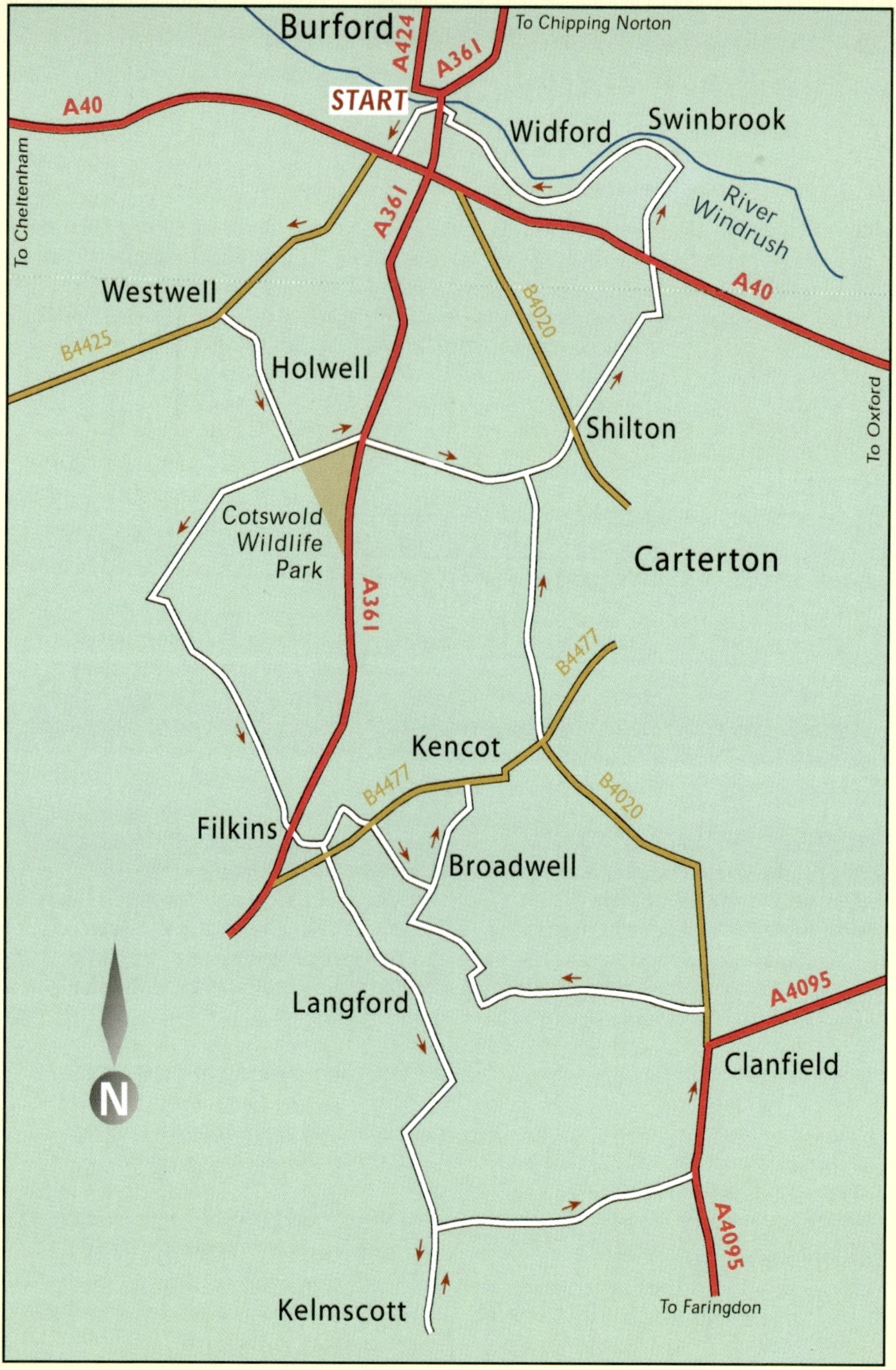

To Chipping Norton

A424

A361

START

A40

To Cheltenham

A361

Widford

Swinbrook

River Windrush

A40

To Oxford

B4020

Westwell

B4425

Holwell

Shilton

Cotswold Wildlife Park

A361

Carterton

B4477

Kencot

B4477

B4020

Filkins

Broadwell

A4095

Langford

Clanfield

N

A4095

Kelmscott

To Faringdon

Widford church seen through the hedge

Westwell) (CARE!). **Turn L** at the T-junction in Westwell (signed Holwell). Ride through Holwell.

(*) **Turn R** at the crossroads (signed Eastleach Martin/Fairford). **Turn L** at the crossroads (signed Filkins/ Lechlade). **Turn R** (signed Filkins). In Filkins **turn L** at the T-junction (not signed). Soon there is a small museum on the left. Then a little further on the Cotswold Woollen Weavers will be seen also on the left.

When you are ready, return to the crossroads (not signed but there is a brick-built bus shelter on the corner) and **turn L**. Go straight over at the crossroads (signed Langford/ Faringdon). Ride through Langford. Cross the disused railway line and then **turn R** opposite Lower Farm (not signed). At the crossroads you have the

option for an excursion to visit Kelmscott (go straight ahead and keep bearing left for the Manor). Otherwise **turn L** (signed Clanfield/Faringdon). **Turn L** at the T-junction (signed Witney/Clanfield A4095). Ride through Clanfield until you get to the far edge of the village. Here **turn L** (signed Broadwell/Calcroft Lane). At the end of this single track road **turn R** at the T-junction (not signed).

(**) Ride through Broadwell and Kencot. In Kencot **turn R** at the crossroads (signed Alvescot/ Bampton/Witney). **Turn L** (signed Carterton, B4477). **Turn L** at the crossroads (signed Shilton). There is a shallow and steady climb to the next road junction. At this T-junction **turn R** (signed Shilton). (***) Ride into the village, the road swings round to the left but straight on is a ford to inspect!

Broadwell church

If not stopping at the ford, carry on round to the left and climb out of the village. Go straight across at the crossroads (not signed), *CARE*.

Turn L at the T-junction (signed Swinbrook/Witney). Take *GREAT CARE* at the next two junctions. **Turn L** at the T-junction onto the A40 (signed Cheltenham/Burford) and soon **turn R** (signed Swinbrook). Descend to the edge of Swinbrook and enjoy the vista on the way down! It is a typical Cotswold scene that changes with the seasons. If you are riding on Sunday afternoon during the summer, cricket will probably be being played on the Swinbrook Cricket Club ground adjacent to the crossroads.

Turn L at the crossroads at the bottom of the descent (signed Widford/Burford). Ride through

Widford then **turn R** at the T-junction (signed Burford). In Burford, **turn R** into the street called Guildenford and follow the road back to the church and the end of the ride.

18-mile route
Follow the 26-mile route as far as the Woollen Weavers in Filkins. On leaving the Woollen Weavers, **turn L** (not signed). **Turn R** on the next left-hand bend onto a single track road (signed Broadwell). Go straight ahead at the staggered crossroads (signed King's Lane). **Turn L** at the T-junction, re-joining the 26-mile route at (**), in Broadwell.

9-mile route
Follow the 26-mile route as far as the crossroads beyond Holwell (*). **Turn L** at this crossroads (signed Shilton). Along this road is the entrance to the Cotswold Wildlife Park (right-hand side). If not visiting the park, then go straight ahead at the crossroads with the A361 (signed Shilton) and rejoin the 26-mile route at (***).

● ●

BURFORD
Burford's history is dominated by the trade in wool and hides which, in the Middle Ages, made its merchants very rich men. They endowed Burford with some magnificent buildings, for example the huge parish church and the Great House, or showed their sense of social responsibility by building almshouses and a school. Local government was in the hands of burgesses who levied tolls to trade, operated the petty law court, made by-laws and assessed the townsfolk for taxes. The Burgesses' Roll, which sets this out, is on view in the Tolsey (the place where trade tolls were collected), now an interesting museum. Entry is free

Fields of oil seed rape near Swinbrook

and it is open April to October, 2 pm to 5 pm. These rights didn't go down well with Sir Lawrence Tanfield who bought the manor in 1617. He was a lawyer, and Chief Baron to the Exchequer to boot, and sued the burgesses, proving that their long-practised rights were illegal. Presumably he then pocketed the tolls and fines himself. When he died, he was so unpopular, he was buried at midnight! Burford achieved notoriety during the Civil War when a group of army levellers were pursued by Royalists into the cellar of the Crown Inn (now a pharmacy) and some were killed.

THE RIVER WINDRUSH
The Windrush is the perfect name for this gentle river that winds some 30 miles from the limestone uplands, where it rises near the hamlet of Cutsdean, to Newbridge where it is subsumed quietly,

without fuss, into the River Thames. It is wonderfully wiggly and alive with wildlife. In one stretch it boasts 8 double S-bends in a mere ¼ mile! The Windrush valley has been inhabited since the Stone Age and in more recent times 17 villages and three towns have sprung up on its banks. Many of the houses in these settlements are built of stone from local quarries which also provided the raw materials for famous buildings further afield, such as some of the Oxford Colleges and St Paul's Cathedral in London. It was also an important factor in the development of the blanket industry in Witney where, according to a local saying, 'it whitens Witney blankets'. Take some time off during your ride to watch the river from one of the stone bridges or picnic along its banks perhaps at Swinbrook, Widford or Burford itself.

Banbury and the Ironstone Villages

18 miles

This route explores several of the pretty ironstone villages in the undulating countryside to the south and west of Banbury. In particular, the route winds through Bloxham, an especially pretty village with a public school, several pubs (including the impressive old coaching inn, the Elephant and Castle), a museum and a wooded corridor (The Gogs) alongside the Bloxham Brook, a perfect place for a picnic on a hot day! The route then heads towards Tadmarton before joining NCN 5 to ride past the old hill fort of Madmarston Hill. It continues to Broughton before coasting down into Banbury using a section of the old Salt Way.

Map: OS Landranger 151 Stratford on Avon, Warwick and Banbury (GR SP462404).

Starting point: Banbury railway station. This is served by trains from London to Birmingham, either from Marylebone (via Bicester) or from Paddington (via Reading and Oxford). There are restrictions on which trains take bicycles, and you may need reservations. If arriving by car, there are plenty of car parks, although all of them are pay and display. We recommend you use one of the large car parks for the Castle Quay shopping centre as these offer easy access to the railway station via the canal towpath. They are well signposted on the approaches to Banbury.

Refreshments: Banbury offers a wide range of restaurants, cafés and pubs. The cafés at the Banbury Museum and at the Mill Arts Centre are both conveniently located along the new canalside development. Along the route there are plenty of pubs at Bloxham, and also at Shutford and Broughton. If you want to enjoy a picnic, then we can recommend investigating The Gogs at Bloxham or The Bretch, just west of the B4035, where NCN route 5 crosses north of Broughton.

The route: This route is fairly hilly, with one or two steepish climbs and descents. However, be prepared to take your time and you will be amply rewarded with some of the prettiest villages and finest pastoral scenery north Oxfordshire has to offer.

Turn **L** out of the station (signed Oxford Canal South) and into a car park. Soon push your bike through a gap in the fence and **turn L** onto the road (signed National Cycle Network 1.75 miles). Soon **turn R** still following blue NCN signs and cross the River Cherwell and the Oxford Canal. **Turn L** at the T-junction (Hightown Road) and soon **turn L** (Bankside). Follow this

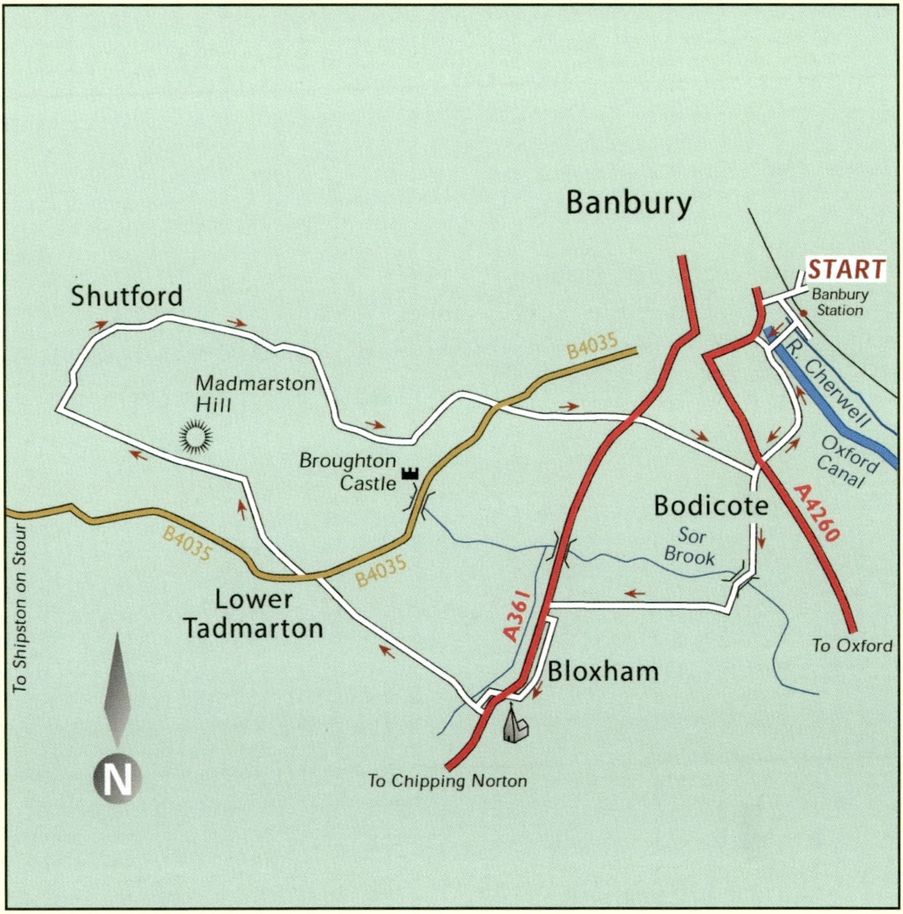

Banbury

START
Banbury
Station

R. Cherwell

B4035

Oxford
Canal

Shutford

Madmarston
Hill

A4260

Broughton
Castle

Bodicote

Sor
Brook

B4035

B4035

To Shipston on Stour

Lower
Tadmarton

A361

To Oxford

Bloxham

To Chipping Norton

N

road, climbing steadily for just over 1 mile. Go straight over at the roundabout (signed Bodicote, NCN 5). Ride through Bodicote and go straight ahead at a 'no through road' sign. Descend carefully (gravel at bottom) and **bear L** to cross the Sor Brook at Bodicote Mill.

Climb the hill, go through the gate next to the barn and then **bear R**. This track soon turns into a quiet surfaced road. Follow this road to within sight of the busy A361. Ride onto a cycle track on the pavement and **turn L** onto

a track beside the A361. **Turn L** (Chipperfield Park Road) and soon **turn R** (Colegrave Road). **Turn R** at the T-junction (signed NCN 5) and soon **turn L** (signed Jubilee Park) and pass the school cricket pitch on the right. **Turn R** at the junction (NOT following NCN 5!) onto Rosebank and follow this narrow road. **Turn L** onto Humber Street and immediately **turn R** (Old Bridge Road). **Turn R** onto the track opposite the Joiners Arms pub and carefully cross the A361. Keep straight ahead (Stoneleigh House on your right) and **bear R** (NCN 5) along Little Green.

![Riding past the windmill at Bloxham Grove]

Riding past the windmill at Bloxham Grove

If you would like to stop and explore The Gogs, then look out for a path to your right. Otherwise continue and **turn R** at the end of Sycamore Terrace, riding between bollards onto a narrow cobbled section of road. Follow this road round and **turn R** at the T-junction (Cumberford Hill), leaving Bloxham behind you.

Turn L at the T-junction in Lower Tadmarton (signed Tadmarton/Shipton on Stour B4035). Descend the hill and **turn R** at the bottom (signed Swalcliffe Lea/Shutford/Edge Hill). **Turn L** in just under 1 mile (signed NCN 5). The old hill fort of Madmarston Hill is the distinctive, flat-topped hill ahead of you and to your right. When the road bends sharp left, keep straight on to a bridle track, still following NCN signs until you meet the road. **Turn R** onto the road (leaving NCN 5). **Turn R** at

the T-junction (signed Shutford/Banbury) and ride through Shutford, following signs for North Newington and Banbury. You will soon find yourself at a junction where five roads meet. Go straight ahead (signed North Newington/Banbury). **Turn R** after approximately 1 mile (signed Broughton). In a while you will see that NCN 5 joins this road from a bridle track on the right. If you wish to visit Broughton Castle or village then **bear R** at the next junction. Otherwise **bear L** following NCN 5 signs and **turn R** at the next T-junction (signed Banbury). Continue on to the T-junction with the B4035.

Turn L onto a pavement cycle track and after about 100 yards, carefully cross the B4035 and follow NCN 5 (signed Banbury) onto a wooded track. Climb a short hill and continue, now

St Mary's church, Banbury

coasting down the track, which is an old Salt Way until it reaches the A361. Cross carefully using the traffic island, and continue following NCN 5 on the other side (signed Banbury). At the next road crossing in Bodicote, **turn L** onto White Post Road. Go straight over at the roundabout onto Bankside and enjoy a long descent into Banbury. **Turn R** at the T-junction at the bottom of Bankside and soon **turn R** (Tramway Road). Cross the canal and the river, and continue following the cycle route signs back to the railway station and the end of the ride.

● ●

BROUGHTON CASTLE

Broughton Castle, the home of the Lords Saye and Sele (the Fiennes family) for 600 years, is a moated manor house located near the village of Broughton, 3 miles south-west of Banbury. It is most famously associated with the Civil War. Before the opening of hostilities, meetings of the Providence Island Trading Company were a front for secret talks among the King's opponents. The castle may be visited from mid May to mid September, Wednesdays and Sundays (also Thursdays in July and August) and Bank Holiday Sundays and Mondays (including Easter) 2 pm to 5 pm. An entrance fee is charged.

BLOXHAM

Bloxham is a pleasant ironstone village which appears to have Anglo-Saxon origins. It is situated on the banks of the Bloxham Brook, a tributary of the River Cherwell. Bloxham hides a dark secret, though. Its church, St Mary's, was partly built by the Devil! At least, it was according to local legend. Its elegant spire is one of the tallest in the county and it also boasts a fine collection of gargoyles, a Norman doorway, medieval paintings and a window by the Pre-Raphaelite artists William Morris and Edward Burne-Jones. There is a small village museum located in the undercroft of the Court House (to the south of the church) which is open every Saturday, Sunday and Bank Holiday from Easter to the end of October, 2.30 pm to 5.30 pm. The old part of the village contains many interesting buildings including the 17th-century inn, the Elephant and Castle, whose car park is accessed through an impressive coaching arch. There are caves under the village. Nobody knows for sure whether these are natural or man-made, but their existence explains why there are plenty of legends about tunnels linking various buildings.

Banbury: Riding through a Civil War Landscape

12 miles

This route takes the Oxford Canal towpath as far as the village of Cropredy, some 4½ miles north of Banbury. For those interested in Civil War history, the first half of the ride takes you through the area over which the battle of Cropredy Bridge was fought in June 1664. Nowadays, you will find it a quiet, unspoilt corner of Oxfordshire and Cropredy itself is a pleasant canalside village best known for the music festival held there every August. At Cropredy the climb out of the Cherwell valley starts, taking us to the hamlet of Williamscot before a short excursion into the neighbouring county of Northamptonshire and the villages of Chacombe and Middleton Cheney. We soon re-enter Oxfordshire and start our descent back to Banbury.

Map: OS Landranger 151 Stratford on Avon, Warwick and Banbury (GR SP462404).

Starting point: Banbury railway station. Banbury is served by trains from London to Birmingham, either from Marylebone (via Bicester) or from Paddington (via Reading and Oxford). There are restrictions on which trains take bicycles, and you may need reservations. If arriving by car, there are plenty of car parks, although all of them are pay and display. We recommend you use one of the large car parks for the Castle Quay shopping centre (see also Route 8). Follow signs to join the route on the canal towpath.

Refreshments: Banbury offers a wide range of restaurants, cafés and pubs. The cafés at the Banbury Museum and at the Mill Arts Centre are both conveniently located along the new canalside development. Along the route there are pubs serving food at Cropredy (the Brasenose Arms) and Chacombe (the George and Dragon). If you prefer to take a picnic, then the village green in Chacombe is a very pleasant spot to choose.

The route: The canal is a contour canal, and so this section of the ride is flat. The sections of canal towpath near Banbury and Cropredy are wide and have a good, even surface. Between this the towpath is a permissive path and the surface is generally either grassy or earthy. It is fine to ride along providing care is taken to look out for uneven surfaces and narrow sections. If you feel unsure, then it is better to get off and walk for a short while. For this reason we do not recommend this route for families with young children or for bikes pulling trailers.

The Oxford Canal at Cropredy

Go more or less straight ahead from the station along the exit road (signed Way Out and Oxford Canal north). Cross over the road at the T-junction (there is a pedestrian crossing to your right) and take the cycle track on the other side (signed Oxford Canal north). **Bear L** almost immediately and ride under a bridge. Follow the path round, **bearing L** past the Art Centre to ride with the canal on your left-hand side. Soon pass the museum and then the Castle Quay car park. Keep straight ahead on the towpath. Ride carefully along the towpath for approximately 4½ miles.

Push your bike up the steep exit ramp immediately before the bridge in the centre of Cropredy. **Turn R** onto the road and soon cross the River Cherwell bridge (the Cropredy Bridge of battle fame). Ride steadily upwards through the hamlet of Williamscot and on to the T-junction with the A361. **Turn R** (signed Banbury) and soon **turn L** (signed Chacombe). **Turn R** at the following T-junction (signed Chacombe) and **turn L** at the next T-junction (signed Middleton Cheney). Ride through the pleasant village of Chacombe, following signs for Middleton Cheney. On leaving the village, climb a steepish hill and go straight over the crossroads with the B4525 and ride into Middleton Cheney.

Go straight ahead at the junction with Main Road into Astrop Road following the blue bicycle route sign to Banbury. Cross the bridge over the A422 and immediately **turn R** onto the cycle track which will take you down and adjacent to the A-road for a couple of hundred yards. Ride through the barrier at the end and back onto a quiet tarmac road (not signed). After cresting a short hill you will be able to see Banbury down in the valley below. Go straight over at the crossroads (signed Overthorpe) and **turn R** at the T-junction (signed Banbury). Descend the steep hill (CARE!) and cross over the M40 on the bridge. Go straight over the first roundabout and get onto the pavement cycle track on the right-hand

To Southam
A423

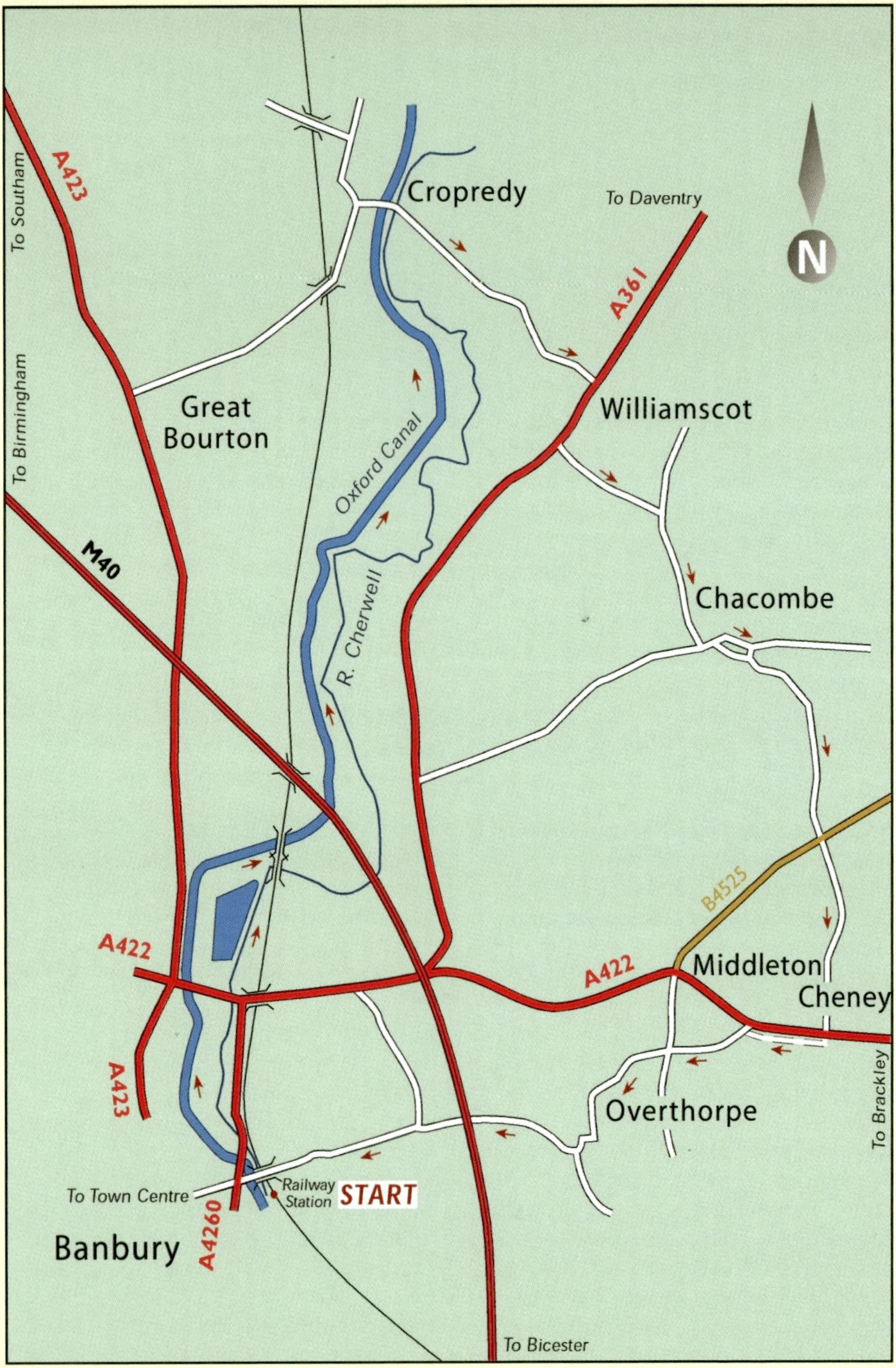

To Birmingham

M40

A422

A423

A4260

Banbury

To Town Centre

Railway Station

START

Cropredy

To Daventry

A361

Williamscot

Great Bourton

Oxford Canal

R. Cherwell

Chacombe

N

B4525

A422

Middleton Cheney

To Brackley

Overthorpe

To Bicester

side of the road immediately before the second roundabout. Use the track to cross Ermont Way and go straight ahead on the track alongside Overthorpe Road. Keep straight ahead through some barriers and get back on the road (Causeway). Follow this and at its end dismount and cross Merton Street using the pedestrian lights. Ride over the railway bridge and **turn L** to return to the station.

If you want to return to the Castle Quay car park, then cross at the pedestrian lights on the railway bridge and take the cycle track (signed Oxford Canal north). Keep left, riding under a bridge and meeting the canal. Ride with the canal on your left. Soon the car park will appear on your right.

● ●

THE OXFORD CANAL

In the early years of the canal boom, the Oxford Canal was one of the most important in the south of England as it joined the Warwickshire coalfields to Banbury and Oxford and also provided a link to the River Thames. It was begun in 1769 by James Brindley who designed it as a contour canal, deliberately following a winding path to minimise the number of locks. The result is that the Oxford to Banbury stretch, 19 miles by road, is 27 miles by canal. It was soon overtaken in importance by the Grand Union Canal linking London and Birmingham. However, the shareholders still made a good return on their investment by dint of charging exorbitant tolls to use the 5½ mile section which linked the Birmingham canal network to the Grand Union Canal. Today life on the Oxford Canal hums to a gentle tune with a pleasing mixture of barges in long-term mooring and leisure craft and plenty of ducks, coots, moorhens, herons,

dabchicks and even the odd water rat to look out for as you ride along.

In Banbury, look out for Tooley's Boatyard which is linked to the new Banbury Museum by a bridge. It contains the oldest dry dock in the country, which dates from 1790 when it was constructed to build and repair the wooden narrowboats that used the new canal. It is still fully operational and tours of the 200-year-old dry dock and forge and other later restored workshops are possible from Easter to the beginning of October on Saturday afternoons at 3 pm, along with short canal trips on a boat built at Tooleys in 2007, *The Dancing Duck*.

CROPREDY BRIDGE

The bridge over the River Cherwell at Cropredy was the site of a pivotal engagement during the English Civil War. In June 1644, the Parliamentary army arrived at Hanwell Castle (north-west of Banbury) while harrying the King's Oxford army. The Royalists marched to meet them but decided not to engage and continued on northwards towards Daventry, taking the east bank of the river. The Parliamentary army, commanded by Waller, shadowed them on the west bank. However, mindful that there were several crossing places of the River Cherwell, and not wanting to be attacked on their flanks, the King ordered his army to march rapidly to secure the bridge at Cropredy. Unfortunately, his rearguard did not receive the order and a mile-long gap opened up. This tempted Waller to cross the Cherwell at Slat Bridge (south of Cropredy) and attack. However, the Royalists were too strong and too determined and although usually described as indecisive, the engagement had lasting repercussions, precipitating the eventual collapse of Waller's army.

Bicester: Flora Thompson Country

16 or 18½ miles

The village of Juniper Hill which features in Flora Thompson's book *Lark Rise to Candleford* is a little way to the north of this route, but her descriptions of rural Oxfordshire life in the late 19th century could just as easily apply to the countryside explored on this ride. From Bicester the route investigates some of the villages to the north of the town, near the border with Buckinghamshire and Northamptonshire.

Map: OS Landranger 164 Oxford, Chipping Norton and Bicester (GR SP585231).

Starting point: The route has three alternative starting points: Bicester North station, Bicester Town station (GR 587219) or Bicester Market Square (GR 586224). Bicester North station is on the Chiltern Trains line between London Marylebone and Birmingham. Bicester Town station serves Oxford and the village of Islip only. There are several bus services from Oxford that will take folding bikes, for example, the X5 (Cambridge) which drops off at Bicester bus station (Bure Place), a short distance from the Market Square. There are two large long-term pay and display car parks on Victoria Road, just to the east of the Market Square.

Refreshments: Bicester has a variety of eating places; however, for a wide range of reasonably-priced food, we recommend the Penny Black located in the old post office in Sheep Street. Along the route, the Butchers Arms in Fringford, the Red Lion in Stratton Audley and the Trigger Pond in Bucknell all serve hot food.

The route: The route doesn't have any hills as such, but you will find that the first half is very slightly uphill, whereas in the second half you will enjoy several gentle descents. If you wish, you can reduce the length of the ride by 3 miles by cutting straight across to Bainton rather than heading to the north through Fringford and Hethe.

Starting from Bicester North station (18½ miles)
Turn **R** out of the station and at the T-junction with the A4421, **turn R** onto the pavement. Ride under the railway bridge and immediately **turn R** onto the cycle track (Town Walk North). At the T-junction at the end of the track, **turn R** onto Balliol Road (following the blue cycle sign). Soon **bear L** onto Keble Rd and **turn R** onto Hertford Close. Exit through the cycle barrier and **turn R** onto the cycle track (Town Walk East). Soon **bear L** and proceed through a tunnel. At the end of the track, cross Maple Road onto

To Buckingham

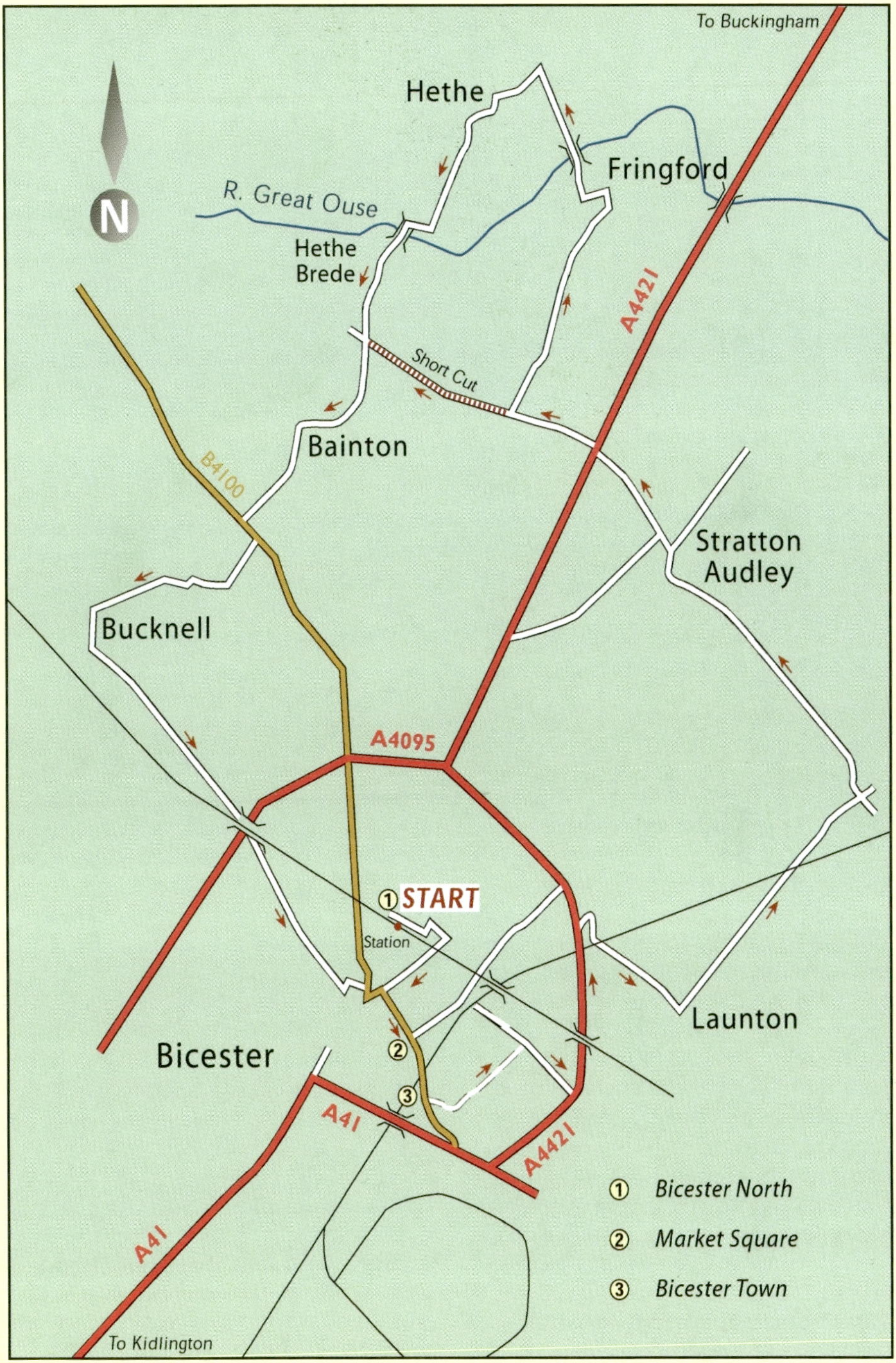

Hethe

Fringford

A4421

R. Great Ouse

Hethe
Brede

Short Cut

B4100

Bainton

**Stratton
Audley**

Bucknell

A4095

① **START**

Station

Launton

Bicester

②

③

A41

A4421

A41

To Kidlington

① *Bicester North*

② *Market Square*

③ *Bicester Town*

N

A magnificent horse chestnut tree at Fringford

Withington Road. Go straight ahead at the 'Give Way' line onto Bell Lane. Dismount your bike and **turn L**, walking through the pedestrian area of Sheep Street to the Market Square.

With your back to Sheep Street (*) (and the HSBC bank to your right) remount and cycle onto the Market Square, following the one-way signs. Exit the square with the Kings Arms Hotel on your right. Go straight ahead at the roundabout (signed Bicester Town station). Cross the railway at the level crossing (**), and turn L at the next roundabout (Mallards Way). After 100 yards, fork right onto a path (following the brown cycle byway sign). **Bear R** keeping the play area to your left. **Turn L** at the T-junction onto the main tarmac track. Keep on this track till the T-junction with the main road. **Turn R** (still following the brown sign). **Turn L** at the ring road roundabout onto the cycle track (signed Launton Village). Take care crossing side roads to the industrial estate and the railway line. As you approach the next roundabout, **turn R**, crossing the ring road and following Sustrans Route 51 signs onto the cycle track. When this track ends (on the railway bridge!), cross carefully and proceed on the road into Launton village.

Turn L at the crossroads in the village centre (Station Road). **Turn L** at the next crossroads (signed Stratton Audley). **Turn L** in Stratton Audley (signed Bicester/Stoke Lyne) with the church on your left. Take care at the staggered crossroads with the A4421.

Turn **R** (signed Buckingham) and immediately **turn L** (not signed). At the next crossroads **turn R** (signed Fringford/Hethe). However, if you wish to take a short cut, go straight ahead at this crossroads (signed Stoke Lyne) and **turn L** (not signed) and rejoin the return route at (+).

In Fringford, **turn L** onto the village green (signed Fringford Only). Soon **turn L** again with the green on your right. **Turn L** at the T-junction at the far end (not signed) and climb gently to meet the Hethe road at a T-junction. **Turn R** (Jubilee Ride sign). **Turn L** after ¾ mile (signed Hethe and Hardwick) and ride through Hethe. **Turn L** (signed Bainton/Stoke Lyne) and soon enjoy a gentle descent to Hethe Brede where you cross the not-so-great Great Ouse, before climbing gently away. At the following crossroads go straight over (not signed) and (+) continue to ride through the ford at Bainton (care!). **Turn L** at the T-junction with the B4100 (signed Bicester) and soon **turn R** (signed Bucknell and Lower Farm barns). In Bucknell, **turn L** at the crossroads (signed Bicester) and enjoy the gentle descent.

On the edge of Bicester go straight over the roundabout (signed to the town centre) and ride under the railway bridge. After ⅓ mile **turn R** onto George Street. Go straight ahead at the crossroads (still George Street) and continue onto the cycle track by the leisure centre. Keep straight ahead till you meet the main road. **Turn L** onto the pavement cycle track and soon cross the road at pedestrian lights. Continue on the cycle track as it passes through a gap in the stone wall ahead of you, across a grassy area, and left, onto a road. Almost immediately

turn **L** back onto the cycle track as it crosses a wooden bridge over a stream. Cross the main road at the traffic island (on your right) and proceed straight ahead, on foot along Wesley Lane. Carefully **turn R** onto Sheep Street.

If you are returning to the Market Square or Bicester Town station, then soon dismount and push your bike through the pedestrian area back to the start. To return to Bicester North station, **bear L** onto Bell Lane and return, following the blue cycle signs, back the way you came at the start.

Starting from Bicester Town station (16 miles)
Turn **R** out of the station following the blue cycle sign (Town Centre). **Turn R** at the T-junction, following the brown cycle byway sign. You have now joined the Bicester North station route at (**). Follow that route.

Starting from the Market Square (16 miles)
Proceed to the northern corner of the Market Square. With Sheep Street behind you and the HSBC bank on your right, join and follow the Bicester North station route from (*).

●●●●●●●●●●●●●●●●●●●●●●●

LARK RISE TO CANDLEFORD
In her trilogy of books, *Lark Rise, Over to Candleford* and *Candleford Green* written between 1939 and 1943, Flora Thompson captured the essence of English rural life at a pivotal time in the 1880s when modern ways of life and thinking were supplanting the old. However, memories of the 'old ways', those of a pre-enclosure England, had not yet been lost from the older generation. The books chart these big social changes through the lives of the

A leafy lane, north of Bicester

inhabitants of Lark Rise (a hamlet), Candleford Green (a village) and Candleford (a small market town). The action is seen through the eyes of Laura, a young woman from Lark Rise as she makes her way through the world. The hamlet of Lark Rise is based on Juniper Hill in north-east Oxfordshire where Flora spent her childhood, just a few miles north of the present route. Many of the villages you will pass through could be imagined to be Candleford Green, villages that were once almost self-sufficient and hummed to the rhythm of nature's own cycles.

Once this whole area was heathland, but that changed when the land was enclosed and put chiefly to corn growing. Juniper, which is a tree of heathland, is now almost extinct from north Oxfordshire. However, there are two trees left at Juniper Hill, to the south of the road through the hamlet, outside the former pub, a reminder of a time now long gone.

The Windrush and Evenlode Valleys

15½ miles

This lovely, quiet circuit gives riders a taster of the countryside around the rivers Windrush and Evenlode. You will soon notice that the gentle, pastoral countryside has many features typical of the Cotswolds: golden stone cottages with slate roofs, cottage gardens and plenty of dry stone walling with its associated flora (moss, ferns and lichen) to admire. The route leaves Witney heading parallel to the River Windrush before climbing out of the valley at Crawley. It then heads through the quiet villages of Delly End, Ramsden and Finstock before descending to the River Evenlode. The wooded climb out of the valley gives interesting views of the river snaking below, especially in the winter when there are no leaves on the trees. The route then continues through East End and on to North Leigh before a gentle descent back to Witney.

Map: OS Landranger 164 Oxford, Chipping Norton and Bicester (GR SP356096).

Starting point: This ride starts from the Buttercross in the centre of Witney, some 11 miles west of Oxford. There is no railway station but if you wish to travel by train, then Hanborough station, which is on the line between Oxford and Worcester, is approximately 1½ miles from the route. Ride west along the cycle track adjacent to the A4095, through Long Hanborough and on to rendezvous with the route at Park Road on the eastern edge of North Leigh. If you travel to Witney by car, there is a free car park on Witan Way, just east off the High Street.

Refreshments: There are numerous cafés and pubs in Witney itself. Along the route, the Woodman in North Leigh, the Lamb in Crawley and the Plough in Finstock all serve food. The Ramsden Garden Centre, which is less than ½ mile from the route, just west of the B4022, has a café which serves both meals and snacks. If the day is a fine one, then both the Roman villa at East End and North Leigh Common are good places to picnic.

The route: The ride is an undulating one, but that is very definitely part of its attraction. All the climbs are on quiet roads, so there is no problem about stopping to admire the view and allowing the pulse to recover!

From Witney's Buttercross, ride west and **turn R** at the mini-roundabout onto High Street (not signed). Go straight over at a mini-roundabout (signed Charlbury/Bicester) and also straight over at the traffic lights with Witan Way. **Turn R** at the next mini-roundabout onto Bridge Street (signed North Witney Industrial Estate) and cross the River Windrush. Soon **turn L**

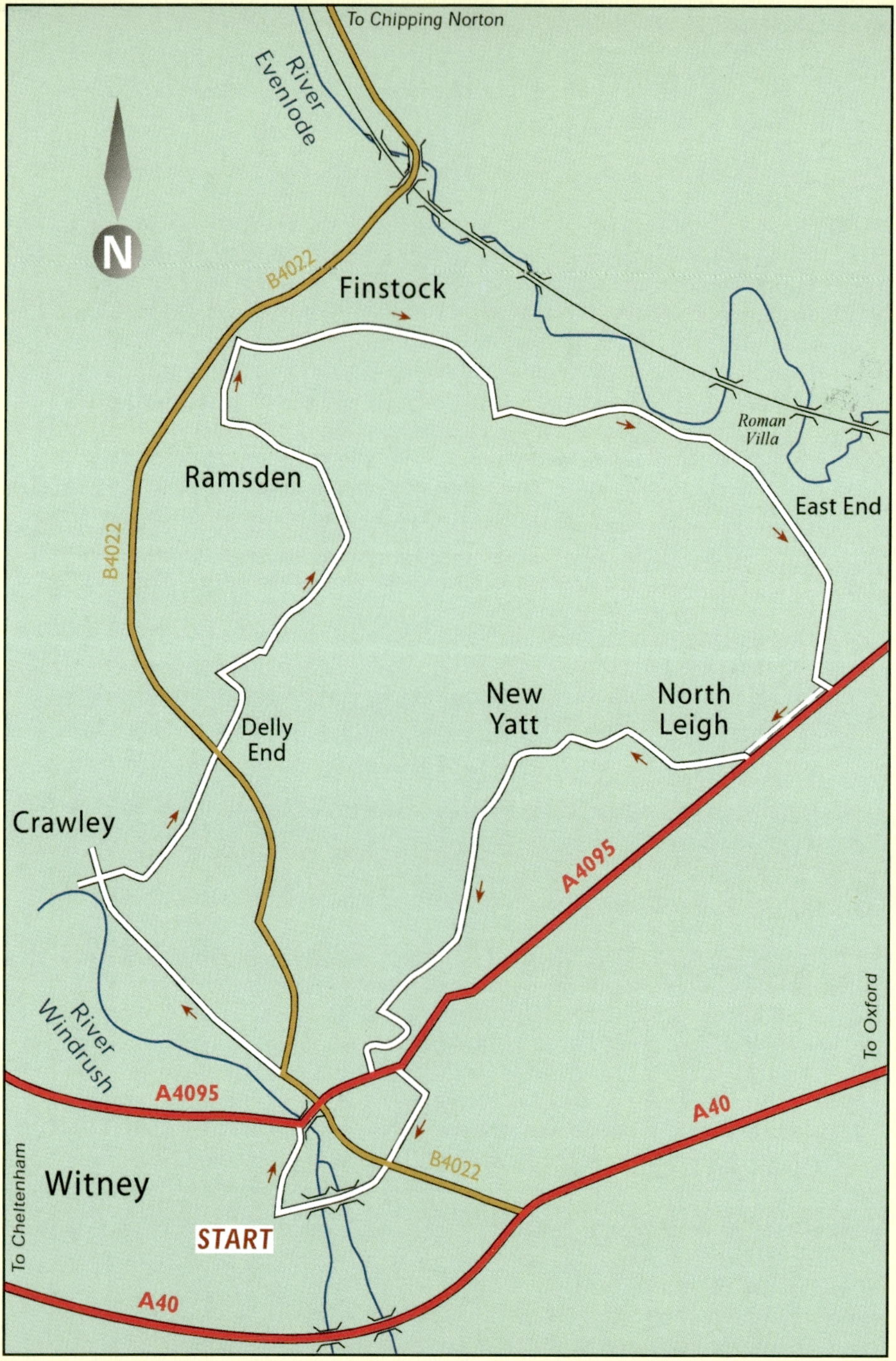

To Chipping Norton

River Evenlode

B4022

N

Finstock

Ramsden

B4022

Roman Villa

East End

Delly End

New Yatt

North Leigh

Crawley

A4095

To Oxford

River Windrush

A4095

B4022

Witney

To Cheltenham

START

A40

A40

Crawley village

at the mini-roundabout onto West End (signed West End Industrial Estate/Hailey). Ride along West End and go straight over at the mini-roundabout onto Crawley Road. Soon leave the town behind and climb gently, enjoying views down to the river on the left. Descend into Crawley and **turn R** at the T-junction (not signed) and keep straight on past the war memorial.

Ride up the hill past the Crawley Inn and at the top, **turn L** (Priest Hill Lane). Go straight over the crossroads with the B4022 (signed Delly End) and keep straight on at the village green (Wood Lane). **Turn L** at the staggered T-junction and ride up and through the village of Ramsden. **Turn R** (signed Mount Skippet) and climb the short

sharp hill. **Turn R** at the T-junction (not signed) and descend the hill into Finstock. Ride through the village, climbing another short sharp hill on exit. **Turn L** at the crossroads (signed East End/Stonesfield) and enjoy a good descent. Take care at the bottom, as you will need to give way at the crossroads! Go straight over at the crossroads (signed East End/ Hanborough).

The road now climbs fairly steeply through woods for about ½ mile. If you can, enjoy the views of the ever-diminishing River Evenlode to your left. Continue straight on and enter East End. The track down to the Roman villa is 100 yards on your left. The villa is situated about ½ mile down this track in a quiet valley, another good

A rural delight

place for a picnic or just a bit of quiet contemplation. Otherwise keep straight on through East End and **turn L** at the T-junction onto Boddington Lane (signed Hanborough, etc.). The small car park on your left just before reaching this junction is for North Leigh Common. Here is another place to stop for a rest, a picnic or to stretch your legs. This common has recently undergone much habitat restoration in order to return it to the wet heathland once typical of much of this part of West Oxfordshire.

Turn **R** onto the cycle track adjacent to the A4095 (signed Witney/North Leigh) and take the **second turn R** onto Park

Road (signed New Yatt, etc.). Ride through North Leigh following signs to New Yatt. Keep straight on, descending gently through New Yatt and onward to the outskirts of Witney. **Turn L** into Early Road and **turn L** again at the T-junction with the A4095. Soon **turn R** (signed Wood Green School, etc.). If the road is busy, there is a handy zebra crossing. Keep left, following the road with 'Farm' written on it and with school railings to the right. **Turn R** onto a track, still keeping the railings to your right about 20 yards before reaching buildings at the end of the road. Continue straight ahead onto a wide gravel track with the school playing field on your right.

Bear **L** to cross a stream on a wooden bridge and immediately **turn R** along a tarmac path which soon brings you out onto the Oxford road. Go straight over into Church Lane. Once again use the zebra crossing if necessary. Keep straight ahead following signs for the town centre. Soon cross the River Windrush on a wooden bridge and **bear L** by an electricity substation to emerge at a roundabout on Witan Way. Go straight over into Langdale Gate (it's easiest to push your bike here) and ride back to the Buttercross.

● ● ● ● ● ● ● ● ● ● ● ● ● ● ● ● ● ● ● ●

WITNEY BLANKETS
The town of Witney in West Oxfordshire is probably best known for its long history of blanket making. It was perfectly situated on the banks of the River Windrush with its supply of water described in 1667 by Dr Robert Plot as the 'abrasive, nutritious water of the River Windrush, wherein they are scored'. It was also located on the edge of the sheep-rearing Cotswolds, from beneath whose beds of oolite Fullers Earth could be extracted for the fulling (or cleansing) process. The company most closely associated with Witney blankets was Charles Early Limited who produced blankets in the town for more than 300 years, only ceasing production in 2002. Originally the entire process was done by hand, but slowly became more mechanised, although as late as 1837 the mills of Witney hummed to water rather than steam power. The company was responsible for setting several 'sheep to blanket' world records. At 4 am on 11th June 1969, 150 sheep from a Cotswold farm were sheared, and completed blankets appeared 8 hours and 11 minutes later! Apparently, one was air freighted to New York and displayed in a shop window on the very same day, quite a feat at the time!

NORTH LEIGH ROMAN VILLA
The Roman villa at North Leigh is one of many in the Cotswolds, often country estates owned and run by wealthy Romano-British families. This particular villa was discovered in 1813 and originally consisted of around 60 rooms arranged in three wings around a central courtyard, including a bath house complex and high status rooms for entertaining. A shelter has been erected over a particularly fine mosaic floor which is believed to have been made by craftsmen from Cirencester. The villa is accessed via a track which would have originally been used by servants, a Roman 'tradesman's entrance'! Entry to the villa is free and it is a wonderfully tranquil place to enjoy a break from cycling.

A Gentle Pedal around the Thames Floodplain

20 miles

Extraction from the floodplain gravels has had a massive impact on the countryside in this part of Oxfordshire and the flooded gravel pits left behind have become an important wildlife resource, especially for over-wintering wildfowl. Don't be surprised to get glimpses of water through the hedgerows as you ride along, or see a grass snake basking on the road! The route leaves Witney to the south along a cycle track into the pleasant village of Ducklington, which is now quiet, having been bypassed by the A415. From there it continues south to the village of Aston where you can make a short detour to visit the pottery. We return to Witney along quiet, narrow lanes through the floodplain villages of Cote, Standlake, Northmoor and Stanton Harcourt.

Map: OS Landranger 164 Oxford, Chipping Norton and Bicester (GR SP356096).

Starting point: This ride starts from the Buttercross in the centre of Witney, some 11 miles west of Oxford. There is no railway station, and the nearest station is Hanborough, 5 miles to the north-east of Witney. If you travel to Witney by car, there is a free car park on Witan Way, just east off the High Street.

Refreshments: There are numerous cafés and pubs in Witney itself. Along the route, the Strickland Arms in Ducklington and the Black Horse in Standlake (just off the route on High Street) are good pubs serving food. Alternatively the Pottery at Aston has a country café serving sandwiches and light lunches, in addition to drinks and cakes. Good spots to picnic along the way are by the village pond in Ducklington, opposite the church in Standlake and by the River Windrush on the cycle track back into Witney. Witney Lakes and Meadow, which are located straight ahead of you immediately after crossing under the A40 on leaving Witney, are also very pleasant to explore.

The route: This is a nice, easy ride on quiet country roads, with only one or two very gentle inclines.

Start at the historic Buttercross in the town centre. Looking towards the church at the end of the green, keep to the left of the Buttercross and follow the road alongside the green and past the church. **Turn R** at the end of the churchyard and ride with the park to your left. Soon **turn L** through the park along an avenue of lime trees. At the end of the path, **turn R** onto the cycle track adjacent to Station Lane and soon cross the road at the pedestrian

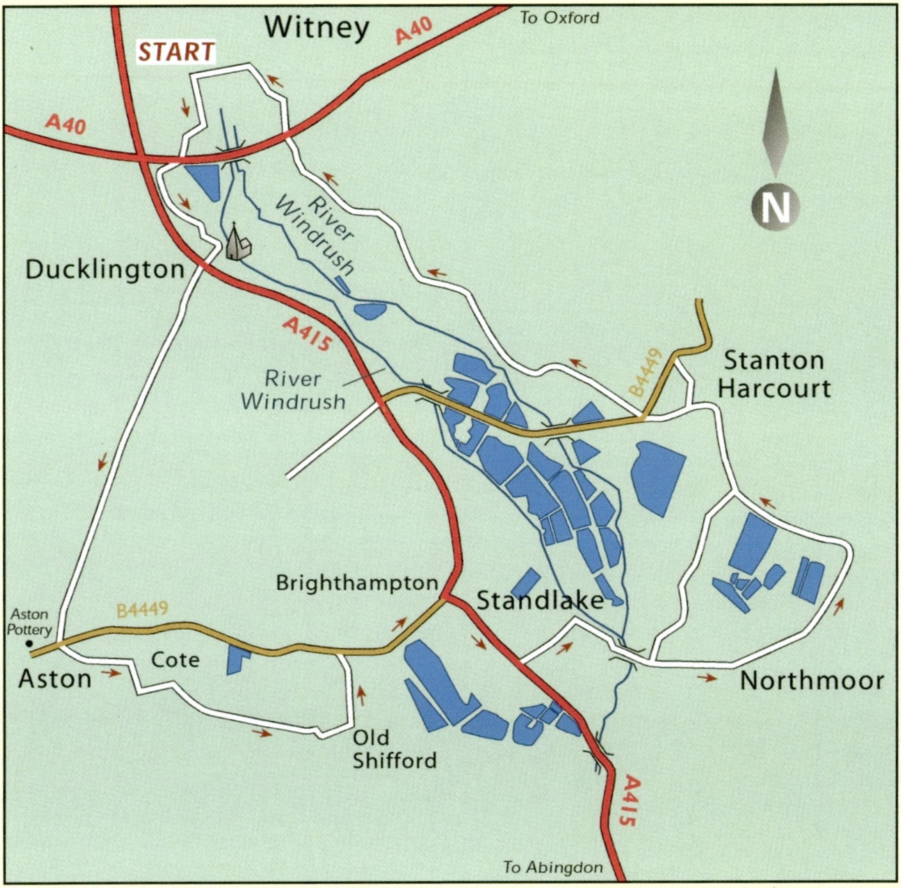

Witney

A40

To Oxford

START

A40

River Windrush

Ducklington

A415

River Windrush

B4449

Stanton Harcourt

Brighthampton

B4449

Standlake

Aston Pottery

Cote

Aston

Old Shifford

Northmoor

A415

To Abingdon

N

crossing. On the other side, **keep R** and soon **turn L** into Station Lane Industrial Estate, Avenue 2. Carry straight on to the end of this road, then join the shared facility. Pass under the A40 and **bear R** over a footbridge. Continue on the cycle track to the roundabout and on to Ducklington.

Ride into the village, then **turn L** onto Church Street. **Bear R** by the church, **turn L** at the T-junction by the war memorial and immediately **turn R** (signed 'Playing Field'). At the end of this road **turn R** at the T-junction with

the A415 (CARE!), then immediately **turn L** (signed Aston). Along some of the slightly elevated sections of this road Aston church can be seen with its distinctive steeple. Keep straight on at the crossroads (signed Aston/Bampton). Ride into Aston. In the centre of the village you can take a little excursion to the pottery: **turn R** at the war memorial (signed Bampton/Faringdon). You will soon see signs for the pottery on your right. On leaving the pottery **turn L** and retrace your steps back to the war memorial, follow the road round (signed Standlake/Cote) and continue below (*).

The popular cycleway in Witney

To continue without visiting the pottery, **turn L** at the war memorial in the centre of the village (signed Standlake/Cote). (*) Soon **turn R** onto Bull Street (signed Chimney, single track road). Ride out of Aston, then **turn L** (signed Cote/Old Shifford). In Cote, **turn R** at the T-junction (signed Old Shifford). Soon you will come to the site of some abandoned cottages, now very overgrown with vegetation and trees. This is the site of Old Shifford. The church is still kept very well maintained. Just outside the entrance porch stand the remains of an early Saxon preaching cross.

Continue along this road and **turn R** at the T-junction (signed Standlake). Ride into Brighthampton and **turn R** onto Abingdon Road (signed Abingdon/ Kingston Bagpuize A415). Ride past the cricket ground (on your left) and soon **turn L** along a well-surfaced bridle track (signed 'Bridleway'). **Turn R** when the track meets the road (not signed). Soon Standlake church will come into

view on the right. The woodwork in the porch is decorated with carvings and in the summer is often used by swallows to nest in. Continue and **turn L** at the village green (signed Village Hall).

Leave Standlake and **turn R** on a left-hand bend (signed Northmoor/Bablock Hythe). In Northmoor, keep straight ahead following signs for Bablock Hythe. A little under a mile beyond the village, **bear L** (signed Stanton Harcourt). The road to your right takes you down to the River Thames and the Ferryman pub. At one time a small ferry took foot passengers (and bikes) across the river but, alas, no more. Continue along the single track road until you reach a T-junction. **Turn R** here (signed Stanton Harcourt/ Eynsham). Ride into Stanton Harcourt. The Manor House and Pope's Tower are on your right and are sometimes open to the public. **Turn L** in the village into Blackditch (signed Industrial Estate). At the end of this road, **turn R** at the

Ducklington village pond

T-junction (signed Hardwick/Eynsham). Soon, **turn L** (signed Bampton/Hardwick), and then **turn R** (signed Cogges).

Cross the A40 on a bridge and enter the outskirts of Witney. **Turn L** soon after the road sign warning of a pedestrian crossing, to join the shared cycle track and footpath (signed Town Centre). Keep straight on at the junction with the road, staying on the path. **Turn L** at the next junction (signed Town Centre). Beware of pedestrians along this popular stretch of path. Cross the River Windrush and keep to the left of the electricity sub-station to emerge at a roundabout on Witan Way. Go straight over into Langdale Gate (it's easiest to push your bike here) and ride back to the Buttercross.

● ●

ASTON POTTERY

Aston Pottery was founded in 1990 and now employs 25 people making kitchen and tableware on the site using traditional techniques. There is a large shop and café and there are also 'decorate your own pottery' sessions every Saturday, should you be feeling artistic.

STANTON HARCOURT

This is a pretty village full of thatched cottages and handsome town houses. The medieval manor house includes a tower, built in 1470, and known as Pope's Tower because the poet Alexander Pope stayed there in 1718 whilst translating Homer. The manor house and grounds are open to the public at regular intervals.

The nearby gravel workings have given scientists a rare insight into the fauna and conditions during one of the interglacial periods some 200,000 years ago. Finds include some 700 bones and teeth of large animals: bison, horse, mammoth, bear and hyena. Some early human tools have also been recovered. All were deposited in silt, sand and gravel by what is thought to have been the ancient Thames at a time when it was confluent with the River Rhine, and Britain was still joined by a land bridge to mainland Europe. The discoveries of mammoths is baffling, firstly because the species found here is much smaller than usual (some of the tusks were still almost 10 ft long!) and, secondly, because the climate during this interglacial was much warmer than would usually support mammoths. Some of the discoveries may be viewed in the Natural History Museum in Oxford.

Faringdon: Arts and Country Crafts

16 or 23 miles

Faringdon, a market town perched on high ground, has many ancient buildings plus the last folly to be built in this country, in 1935. This well-known local landmark, which even once starred in an episode of *The Avengers*, is located just north-east of the town and is worth visiting. The rides start in the Market Place which is dominated by the old town hall building and there is a choice of routes. On the 23-mile route we will visit Filkins, home to the Cotswold Woollen Weavers. Both routes offer the possibility of two short detours. Why not explore the peaceful Thameside village of Kelmscott? The Manor House, where William Morris once lived, is sometimes open to the public. There is also St John's Lock where the sculpture depicting Old Father Thames resides. The routes then go to Coleshill, and as we approach the village there are views of the wind turbines at Watchfield. After climbing Badbury Hill (National Trust) there are great views across Oxfordshire to enjoy. Towards the end of the ride we visit the Great Barn (National Trust) in Great Coxwell.

Map: OS Landranger 163 Cheltenham and Cirencester (GR SU289956).

Starting point: Both rides start in the Market Place in the centre of Faringdon, some 17 miles south-west of Oxford and 10 miles north-east of Swindon on the A417. Faringdon is not on the rail network. The nearest station is at Swindon. If you arrive by car, we recommend you park in the Southampton Street car park. From the Market Square, take the road by the Bell Hotel and the car park is soon on your right. It is a pay and display car park, but free on Sundays.

Refreshments: There are several pubs in Faringdon, including the Bell Hotel and the Crown coaching inn, both in the Market Square. Along the route there are pubs at Alvescot (the Plough), Langford (the Bell), and the Trout near St John's Lock on the A417, that serve food. There is also a café at the Woollen Weavers at Filkins when the museum is open. Lechlade, a short distance from the route, has several cafés and pubs to choose from.

The route: The routes are predominantly flat as they mostly pass through the floodplain of the River Thames. However, be prepared for a single steep climb out of Coleshill. There is much to visit and explore on these routes, so make sure you give yourself plenty of time.

23-mile route
Head out of the Market Place, north and towards the church (signed Witney A4095). Just after the church **turn L** (signed Witney/Radcot/Clanfield). Cycle through Radcot, crossing the

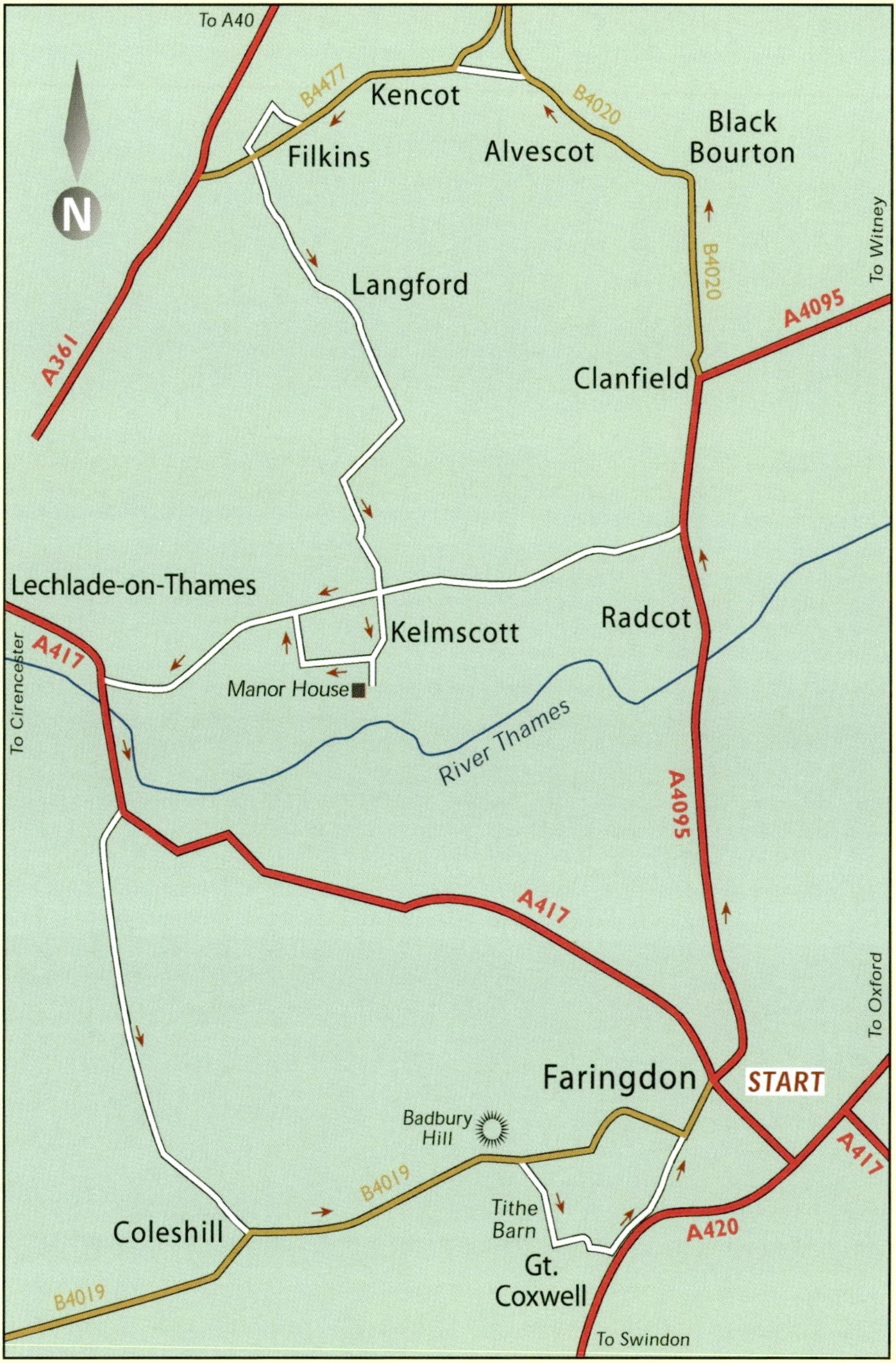

To A40

B4477

Kencot

B4020

Filkins

Alvescot

Black Bourton

N

To Witney

A361

Langford

B4020

Clanfield

A4095

Lechlade-on-Thames

Kelmscott

Radcot

To Cirencester

A417

Manor House

River Thames

A4095

A417

To Oxford

Faringdon

START

A417

Badbury Hill

A420

Coleshill

B4019

Tithe Barn

Gt. Coxwell

B4019

To Swindon

The Tithe Barn at Great Coxwell

River Thames and keep straight ahead for Clanfield. Cycle through Clanfield straight ahead on the B4020 (signed Carterton/Burford) when the A4095 turns off to the right in the village. Continue on to Black Bourton, where you keep straight on (signed to Burford). Cycle through Alvescot. Just after leaving Alvescot **turn L** (signed Kencot/Filkins). Take care; the sign is partly obscured by trees. In Kencot keep straight ahead at the crossroads (signed Filkins/Lechlade).

Turn R at the staggered crossroads (not signed, but a left turning is signposted to Kings Lane). Ride along this single track road into Filkins village. **Turn L** at the T-junction (not signed). The Cotswold Woollen Weavers are soon on the right. When you are ready, continue through the village. You will pass a small museum of rural life (the Swinford Museum, open the first Sunday of the month, April to September) on your right. **Turn L** at the crossroads (not signed). There

is a brick-built bus shelter on the corner.

Go straight on at the crossroads (signed Langford/Faringdon) and cycle through the lovely village of Langford. The church, with its Saxon tower, is well worth a visit. Cross the disused railway and **turn R** opposite Lower Farm (not signed). If you wish to visit peaceful Kelmscott with its associations with the Arts and Crafts movement, go straight over at the next crossroads and keep bearing left for the Manor House. We recommend that you return to the route by looping through the village, turning left near the church and rejoining the route by turning left at the T-junction. The entire detour is about 1½ miles.

If you don't detour, **turn R** at the crossroads (*) (signed Little Faringdon/ Lechlade). Another detour presents itself at the T-junction with the A417. **Turn L** (signed Faringdon). St John's Lock, the highest on the Thames, is a

short distance on your right. Why not enjoy a short break here and visit Old Father Thames or wet your whistle in the Trout pub on the other side of the road? When you are ready, continue along the A417, taking care on this short stretch of busy road.

Soon **turn R** (signed Coleshill). Take care as the turning is on a bend in the road. Ride through Coleshill until you reach the T-junction with the B4019. **Turn L** (not signed). Soon the road descends from Coleshill, then rises steeply to Badbury Hill. This is a National Trust site. Descend with care as we are going to make a right-hand turn before the full descent. **Turn R** at the crossroads (signed Great Coxwell Tithe Barn/Village Only). Take care on this narrow road which descends quite steeply. As the road levels out, the Tithe Barn (National Trust) comes into view on the right.

The barn is well worth a visit and when you are ready, continue into the village of Great Coxwell. Soon **turn L** opposite Holloway House (not signed). Go straight ahead at the mini-roundabout (signed Faringdon). Keep straight on, then **turn L** at the next mini-roundabout onto Gravel Walk (signed Lechlade/Witney). **Turn R** onto Gloucester Street (signed Witney/Town Centre). Continue until back in the Market Place, and the end of the ride.

16-mile route

Ride out of Faringdon on the 23-mile route as far as Radcot. Cross the River Thames and **turn L** after about ¾ mile (signed Kelmscott). Stay on this road until the T-junction with the A417. You will rejoin the 23-mile route at the crossroads (*).

KELMSCOTT

Kelmscott is a pleasant stone-built village lying on the Thames floodplain. Its sense of remoteness is compounded by its position at the end of a single track road leading only to the village. The village is best remembered for William Morris, the craftsman, social philosopher and poet who lived here in the Elizabethan stone manor house from 1871 till his death in 1896. The Manor House, which he described as a 'heaven on earth', is now owned by the Society of Antiquities and is open to the public. An entrance fee is charged. On your way back through the village, look out for the relief of William Morris, in artistic pose, on the wall of Morris Cottages, built at the expense of his widow in 1902.

GREAT COXWELL BARN

The barn at Great Coxwell is a cathedral of a building. It was completed sometime in the mid 13th century for the Cistercian monks of Beaulieu Abbey (in Hampshire) who had been granted the manor of Faringdon in 1204 by King John. The barn would have stored the produce of the Grange (a large farm) which once provided vital income for the abbey. The dimensions speak for themselves: 152 ft in length, 44 ft in width with a gable height of 48 ft. The roof, which is beautifully tiled in Cotswold slate, is supported by two rows of oak posts on top of 7ft-high stone pillars. It is amazing that after more than 700 years of resisting the pressures from the roof, all are original and, what's more, not one has shifted in position. There is a dovecot over the east door, and originally there would have been a loft in the west porch, accommodation for the brother in charge of the barn (the grangerius). The barn is now in the care of the National Trust, and there is a small entrance fee. It is open daily between dawn and dusk.

14

Abingdon and the Distant Dreaming Spires

10 or 19 miles

This figure-of-eight circuit starts and finishes in Abingdon's Market Square and winds its way around Albert Park before heading north to the village of Sunningwell. For the more energetic, a short but sharp climb up to Boars Hill awaits. The rewards are splendid views over the 'dreaming spires' of Oxford and the chance to explore Jarn Mound, with its garden and viewpoint designed by the well-known archaeologist Sir Arthur Evans and its literary connections to Matthew Arnold. The route continues downhill to Wootton and Dry Sandford. Why not take some time to explore the nature reserve of Dry Sandford Pit which has much to offer of geological and wildlife interest? This part of Oxfordshire is well known for its calcareous fens which are home to much rare wildlife. We then skirt the edge of Abingdon airfield before joining up with the 10-mile route back in Sunningwell and Abingdon.

Map: OS Landranger 164 Oxford, Chipping Norton and Bicester (GR SU498971).

Starting point: The Market Square in the centre of Abingdon There are two car parks (pay and display) immediately south of the river bridge on the A415 at Abingdon, 8 miles south of Oxford. The town cannot be reached by train. The nearest railway station is Radley, 3 miles away, on the line between Oxford and Didcot. If you travel by train, you may pick up the route outside Radley station with a simple turn L out of the station.

Refreshments: There are several cafés in the main square at Abingdon and Zeko's Café in Bath Street. In summer, drinks and ice creams are also usually available from a kiosk in the Abbey Meadows. Along the route, the Flowing Well in Sunningwell, the Bystander in Wootton and the Bowyer Arms in Radley all serve food. Alternatively, why not carry a picnic and eat al fresco looking down on the 'dreaming spires' from Boars Hill?

The route: The 19-mile route contains one short but stiff climb, but is otherwise only gently undulating. The 10-mile route incorporates mostly flat, gentle riding. Both include sections on tracks and bridleways, all of which have a good surface.

19- and 10-mile routes

From Abingdon Market Square, head west along High Street. Keep straight ahead past the war memorial. Go straight ahead at the traffic lights (signed A34, All Other Routes). Soon

To Oxford

A4144

A423

A34

N

Jarn
Mound — Boars
Hill

Wootton

Bayworth

Sunningwell

Dry
Sandford

x

Dry
Sandford
Pit

B4017

Cothill
Fen

Radley

Airfield

Stn.

A4183

Gozzard's
Ford

Shippon

A415

A415

START — River Thames

Abingdon

To Kingston Bagpuize

River Ock

A34

To Didcot

Abingdon's 17th-century county hall

turn R onto Conduit Road (signed Carswell School). Go straight ahead at the crossroads (Park Crescent) and ride with Albert Park on your left. **Turn R** opposite the statue of Prince Albert and ride between bollards. **Turn R** onto Faringdon Road (not signed). **Turn L** at the mini-roundabout (signed Wootton/ Cumnor). Go straight on at the next mini-roundabout and very soon **turn R** at traffic lights onto Northcourt Road.

Turn L onto Sellwood Road. Soon **turn R** at the T-junction (still Sellwood Road). **Turn L** onto Holland Road and **turn R** at the T-junction onto South Avenue. **Turn L** at the next T-junction (still South Avenue) and where the road ends, join the cycle track by riding through the barriers. Continue and go straight ahead, crossing Boulter Drive. Exit through the gate and carefully cross the road. Go through the gate and continue on the stony track which

crosses the A34 on a bridge. When you emerge near some buildings, keep straight on and **turn R** back onto the road (not signed). If you wish to ride the 19-mile route, then **turn L** (signed Bayworth), otherwise continue straight on, rejoining the longer route instructions at (*).

19-mile route only
Turn R at the T-junction in Bayworth onto Brumcombe Lane (signed Boars Hill). Soon you will find yourself climbing and before long the gradient gets quite steep. Luckily, it's only a short climb so get off and walk if you prefer. **Turn L** at the T-junction at the top (signed Cothill, etc.) **Turn R** onto Berkeley Road (signed Old Boars Hill). To your right are fields bought by the Oxford Preservation Trust to ensure the survival of the 'dreaming spires' view. On a clear day, it's a great place for a picnic. When you're ready, continue on past Rippon Hall (Open University) and **bear L** (signed Jarn Way, etc.) After about ½ mile, the road bends left sharply and heads downhill. On your right is Jarn Mound and gardens, another spot for a picnic. Matthew Arnold's Field is straight ahead along a track. There is an information board and map which will help you in your explorations.

To continue, **turn L** and carefully descend the hill (signed Old Boars Hill). **Turn L** at the next T-junction (signed Lower Wootton). **Turn R** at the T-junction (Lamborough Hill) and immediately **turn L** onto Besselsleigh Road (signed Besselsleigh). Turn immediately onto the pavement and follow the bridle track with the playing field to your left. This track soon emerges in Lansdowne Road. **Turn L** at the T-junction (not signed) and **turn R**

at the next T-junction onto Cothill Road (signed Cothill, etc.). If you want to stop and explore the Dry Sandford Pit nature reserve, the entrance is 100 yards on your left. Otherwise, keep straight on into Cothill. Cothill Fen can be visited by walking down the path opposite the Merry Miller pub. When you are ready, continue on past the pub and **turn L** on the outskirts (signed Shippon, etc.). **Turn L** at the T-junction in Gozzards Ford (signed Shippon, etc.). Just opposite this turn there is a very handsome milestone which helpfully informs you that you are 58 miles from London!

Soon you will find yourself riding along the edge of Abingdon airfield. **Turn L** (signed Shippon and Dalton Barracks). Ride past the entrance to the barracks and on through the old part of Shippon. If you decide that you want to return to Abingdon quickly, **turn R** at this T-junction; Abingdon is 1 mile away, over the A34 bridge. However, to enjoy the full ride and a more scenic return, **turn L** instead (signed Sunningwell). **Turn L** at the next T-junction onto the B4017 for ¼ mile and then carefully **turn R** onto Sunningwell Road (signed Sunningwell). Ride through the village, **bearing R** by the Flowing Well pub. Soon you will pass the end of Pen Lane again. However, this time keep straight on rather than turning for Bayworth.

Both routes
(*) Go straight on at the staggered crossroads onto Sugworth Lane. Enjoy a gentle descent for a mile or so. After a while you will have Bagley Wood on your left. Here there are plenty of footpaths to explore and in late April and May this is one of the best places to come and see bluebells. **Turn R** at

the T-junction and on to the pavement cycle track (signed Radley). Join the road after ½ mile. Pass the entrance to Radley College and **turn L** onto Church Road (signed Station). Continue through the village. Pass the railway station and on leaving the village, **turn L** (Thrupp Lane, NCN Route 5). **Bear R** by the aggregate quarry and soon **turn L** (signed Abingdon NCN Route 5). Continue on a track with lakes on both sides. **Bear R** through some barriers and keep following NCN Route 5. After about 1 mile, cross the Abbey Stream on a wooden bridge and **turn R** along the stream. Re-cross on the second (wooden) bridge and **turn L** (signed Sustrans Cycle Route) through a car park and onto Abbey Close. You will see some of the few remains of Abingdon Abbey in the meadow to your right. Bear left under the Abbey Gateway and the Market Square is ahead and to your right.

ABINGDON
The market town of Abingdon is the site of the oldest continually occupied settlement in England. Excavations show that it has been inhabited for 6,000 years. For many years Abingdon was the county town of Berkshire and, as such, held assizes in the Old County Hall. This elegant building built around 1680 by Christopher Kempster still shelters the weekly market and houses the local museum. On important royal occasions it is the centre of a tradition, unique to Abingdon – bun throwing.

JARN MOUND
Jarn Mound, and much of the surrounding area, is now looked after by the Oxford Preservation Trust. The Mound itself is artificial and was built between 1929 and 1931. It was the brainchild of Sir Arthur Evans, the well-known archaeologist, who lived locally and wanted to ensure that the view of the 'dreaming spires' of Oxford was preserved, at a time when other views of it were threatened with development. He also oversaw the preservation of Matthew Arnold's Field so that the landscape which inspired the poet and appeared in *Thyrsis* and in *The Scholar Gypsy* would not be lost. Today, the area is criss-crossed with numerous paths and is a very pleasant place to wander around, or to rest after climbing the hill.

COTHILL FEN
Cothill Fen is one of the most species-rich lowland calcareous fens in the UK and as such has been designated a Site of Special Scientific Interest (SSSI), and part of it is also a National Nature Reserve (NNR). There are two nature reserves (Cothill Fen and Parsonage Moor) to explore, both a short walk down an old track called String Lane, opposite the Merry Miller pub in the village of Cothill. They are host to numerous rare plants including marsh helleborine and grass of Parnassus and a variety of other wildlife.

15

Wantage and the Vale of White Horse

23 miles with optional 5-mile detour to climb White Horse Hill

From alongside the statue of King Alfred in the Market Square in Wantage, this route leaves the town in an easterly direction to explore the villages of East and West Lockinge, home to several horse-racing stables. It then descends into the Vale of White Horse and passes through the pleasant villages of East and West Hanney and Denchworth before emerging onto the large village common at Goosey, where the Berkshire Downs come into view. At Uffington the main route heads up to Kingston Lisle and turns east on tiny roads and tracks through Westcot, Sparsholt, Childrey and East Challow, before returning to Wantage. For the more adventurous a 5-mile detour offers the opportunity to explore the large village of Uffington, with its octagonal church tower, Tom Brown's School Museum and pleasant brick and chalk-faced cottages. It also offers the challenge of a climb up White Horse Hill. The views from the top are splendid, and on a fine day it's a grand location for a picnic.

Map: OS Landranger 174 Newbury and Wantage (GR SU398879).

Starting point: The route starts from the Market Square in Wantage, which is located on the A417, some 10 miles west of Didcot. There is short-term parking in the Market Square, but for long-term parking we recommend using the pay and display car park off the B4507 (Portway) to the south of the Market Square. Toilets are available here, and parking is free on a Sunday. To get to the Market Square from the car park, exit with the Civic Centre on your left. **Turn L** onto Portway and **turn L** again at the traffic lights (signed Town Centre). This road will lead you to the square.

Refreshments: There are plenty of refreshment opportunities along this route. The Fox at Denchworth, the Plough at West Hanney, the Fox and Hounds at Uffington, the White Horse at Woolstone and the Blowingstone at Kingston Lisle all serve food. Alternatively, a short detour into Ardington village brings you to Smith's Bistro at the post office and village store.

The route: This is an undulating and varied route with a steep hill at Kingston Lisle, but the optional detour up to White Horse Hill is strictly for the energetic and is quite a challenge, though surely the most spectacular climb in Oxfordshire.

23-mile route

To leave Wantage Market Square, ride clockwise round the square and exit onto the A417 (signed Reading, A417). **Turn R** at the roundabout (signed Reading, A417) and keep straight ahead at the next two mini-roundabouts, still following signs to Reading. Soon **turn R** up Springfield Road. After a while **turn L**, still Springfield Road. **Turn L** at the T-junction (not signed) and soon **turn R** onto a tarmac track (signed Harwell Campus/Didcot Route 44). Ride along this track and when it meets the road **bear R** onto the road (Route 44). **Turn L** at the T-junction (signed Ardington), leaving Route 44 at this point. Continue on this road till it meets the A417. Go straight over at the A417 crossroads and descend the hill into the Vale of White Horse.

Turn R onto the A338 (signed East Hanney). Take care along this short stretch of main road. **Turn L** after a mile (signed West Hanney/ Denchworth, etc.) and ride through the village following signs for West Hanney. Ride into West Hanney. If you would like to explore the church or visit the Plough pub, then **turn L** by the war memorial (signed to the church), otherwise continue straight ahead (signed Denchworth). In Denchworth keep straight ahead (signed Goosey) and soon bear sharp right by the Fox pub (signed Challow/Stanford in the Vale). Soon after leaving the village, **turn R** (signed Goosey). **Turn L** at the T-junction (signed Goosey, etc.). Ride through Goosey with its large village common, small church and views of the Berkshire Downs beyond.

Continue and, at the T-junction with the A417, **turn R** (signed Faringdon) and soon **turn L** (signed Uffington/Baulking). **Bear L** in the small hamlet of Baulking (signed Uffington). **Turn L** at the T-junction on the edge of Uffington (signed Fawler/Kingston Lisle)(*).

Ride through Fawler and climb the steep hill into Kingston Lisle. **Bear R** in the village (signed Wantage/Lambourn) and continue on to the crossroads with the B4507. For those of you who want to try their luck waking King Alfred, the Blowingstone can be visited in the garden of a cottage straight ahead a few hundred yards across the B4507! Otherwise, **turn L** (signed Wantage) along the B4507. **Turn L** (signed Westcot) and follow the road down and through the village. **Turn L** at the T-junction (signed Sparsholt) and **turn L** at the next T-junction in Sparsholt (opposite the church). Soon **turn R** (signed Childrey).

Turn R at the T-junction (signed Childrey) and ride into the village, passing the Reading Room and village pond, both on your left. **Turn L** by the Hatchett pub (Stow Hill) and turn up a tarmac bridlepath between houses (signed as a No Through Road) and climb gently. Go straight across, still on a track where it crosses the minor road. Enter East Challow passing a school on your left and **turn R** onto Windmill Place. Take the second **turn L** (High View) and **turn R** at the T-junction opposite the cricket ground (Vicarage Hill). **Turn L** back onto the B4507 (not signed) and coast gently down into Wantage.

Turn L onto Ham Road (signed Oxford/Grove A338) and soon **turn R** onto Locks Lane. Descend carefully as there is a deep ford at the bottom.

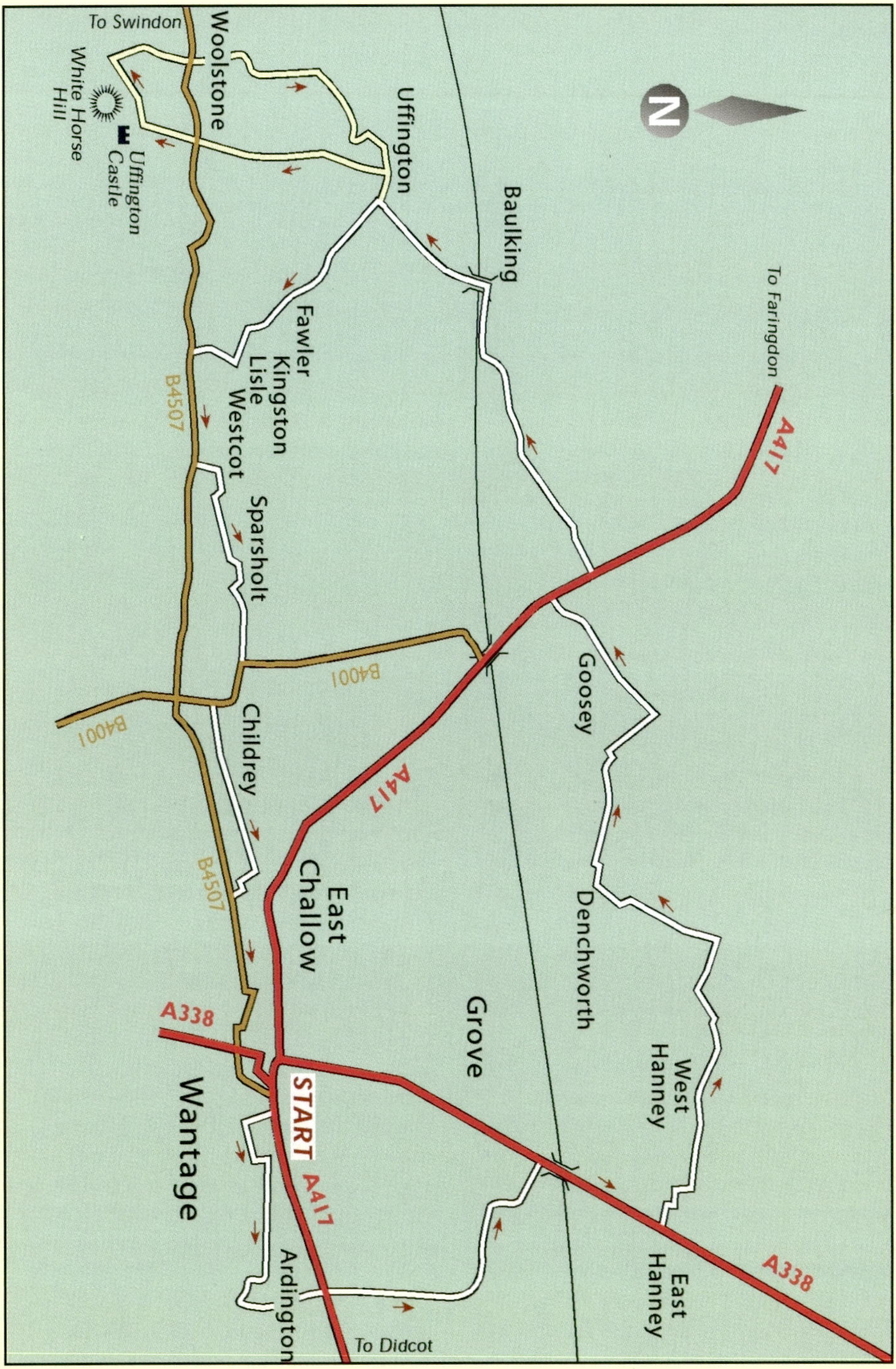
To Swindon
Woolstone
White Horse Hill
Uffington Castle
Uffington
Baulking
N
To Faringdon
A417
Fawler
Kingston Lisle
Westcot
B4507
Sparsholt
B4001
B4001
Goosey
Childrey
A417
East Challow
B4507
Denchworth
Grove
A338
West Hanney
Wantage
START
A417
Ardington
To Didcot
East Hanney
A338

The Manger at White Horse Hill

Cross the ford on the footbridge and continue up Locks Lane following the one-way system. **Turn L** onto Portway. The turning to the car park is soon on your left. To return to the Market Square, follow Portway and **turn L** at the traffic lights (signed Town Centre, etc.) and follow the road back to the square.

5-mile detour to climb White Horse Hill

(*) Leave the main route at the Fawler turning and **turn R** (signed White Horse Hill) and enter Uffington. Soon **turn L** (High Street). Pass the Fox and Hounds pub and soon **turn L** onto Shotover (signed White Horse Hill). Soon you will find the road kicking upwards through a wooded section and you will emerge into the open and reach a crossroads with the B4507. Go straight ahead (not signed) and climb

the hill! Take care on the cattle grids. Take your time and enjoy the views that unfold before you. This road is usually very quiet because the motor traffic is sent up via another route to the National Trust car park. When you are ready, start the descent, crossing two cattle grids. If you would like to make a short excursion to visit the prehistoric long barrow known as Wayland's Smithy, then **turn L** along the track, otherwise **turn R** following signs to the car park and take care descending the steep hill. Go straight ahead at the crossroads at the bottom (signed Woolstone). **Turn R** at the T-junction in the village, next to the White Horse pub (signed Uffington) and follow the Uffington Brook back towards the village. **Turn R** at the T-junction (signed Uffington) and re-enter the village. **Turn L** at the T-junction (signed Fernham) and soon

Relaxing by Childrey village pond

bear R by Tom Brown's School Museum. Continue through the village to rejoin the main route where you left it, at (*).

● ●

WHITE HORSE HILL
The White Horse is an icon of the British landscape, and all the more amazing when you get up close to it and wonder how its elegantly simple form was created when it can only be seen properly from a distance of about a mile! We now know that it was constructed by digging an earth trench that was filled in with chalk blocks. Tests on soil from the base of one such trench showed that it was older than previously thought and dated from the late Bronze Age, around 1000 BC.

WANTAGE
There's no mistaking who is Wantage's favourite son. The statue of King Alfred, who was born in the town in AD 849, dominates the market square of this small town, in what locals sometimes refer to as 'occupied Berkshire'. Wantage is also proud of the poet John Betjeman who lived in the town for many years and wrote several poems about it, including *Wantage Bells* and *On Leaving Wantage*. He has a more modest statue in the Betjeman Memorial Park, a short distance from the church. The Vale and Downland Museum in Church Street is well worth a visit (open all year, Monday to Saturday, 10 am to 4 pm; an entrance fee is charged) and has both permanent and temporary displays about the history and cultural heritage of the Vale of White Horse.

Wantage and the Ridgeway

10 miles

There are spectacular views on this ride, which starts by the statue of King Alfred in the Market Square in Wantage and goes south to the attractive village of Letcombe Regis which lies along the lovely Letcombe Brook. It then heads to the Ridgeway, some 360 ft above the village. The effort is worth it because you will emerge in the middle of the Iron Age hill fort of Segsbury. Cross the far ring ditch and you will reach the Ridgeway itself. On a clear day the views back into the Vale of White Horse and beyond are fantastic. The route then heads west along the Ridgeway before descending into the picturesque village of Letcombe Bassett. A short climb out of the village is followed by a descent into Childrey, where we pick up a track to East Challow and then return on-road to Wantage.

Map: OS Landranger 174 Newbury and Wantage (GR SU398879).

Starting point: The route starts from the Market Square in Wantage, which is located on the A417, some 10 miles west of Didcot. There is short-term parking in the Market Square, but for long-term parking we recommend using the pay and display car park off the B4507 (Portway) to the south of the Market Square. Toilets are available here, and parking is free on a Sunday. To get to the Market Square from the car park, exit with the Civic Centre on your left. **Turn L** onto Portway and **turn L** again at the traffic lights (signed Town Centre). This road will lead you to the square.

Refreshments: The Greyhound Inn in Letcombe Regis serves food, but if the weather is good we suggest that the best option is to carry a picnic to eat either at Segsbury Castle or somewhere up on the Ridgeway. If it's a bit windy (not unknown!) descend the hill and spend some time exploring Letcombe Bassett which is full of interesting old cottages, including Arabella's Cottage, featured in Thomas Hardy's novel, *Jude the Obscure*.

The route: This route is short but hilly with one long and very steep climb from Letcombe Regis to the Ridgeway. Don't let this put you off, you can always push your bike and the effort is amply rewarded with spectacular views. The Ridgeway is a restricted byway which means that on-road vehicles are allowed to use it during the summer months. However, in our experience this shouldn't present any problem as usage isn't very high on this section.

To leave Wantage Market Square, ride clockwise round the square and leave to the west following the 'Through Traffic' sign (Mill Street). **Turn L** at the next mini-roundabout (signed Ashbury B4507). **Turn R** at the T-junction

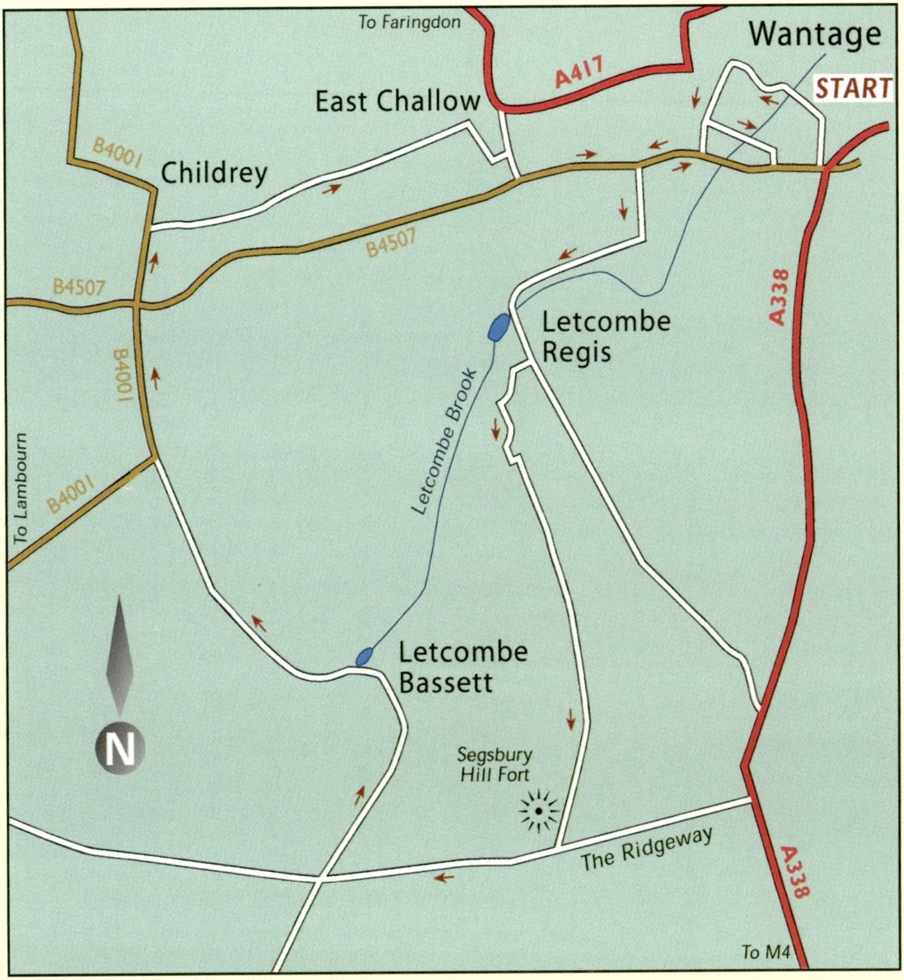

To Faringdon

Wantage

START

A417

East Challow

B4001

Childrey

B4507

B4507

B4001

B4001

To Lambourn

Letcombe Regis

Letcombe Brook

A338

Letcombe Bassett

N

Segsbury Hill Fort

The Ridgeway

A338

To M4

(signed Ashbury B4507) and soon **turn L** (signed Letcombe Regis, etc.). Ride into Letcombe Regis and follow the main road as it twists and turns through the village. **Turn L** near the church, where the road bends sharp right (signed Village and Downs Only). After about 1 mile you will come to the very steep part of the climb. Keep on up and where the gradient flattens out you will see that you are inside the hill fort, surrounded by a large ditch and bank. You will get better views of the

defensive ditch and bank when you cross it again on your way to meet the Ridgeway.

Turn R onto the Ridgeway. After nearly 1 mile a tarmac road crosses the track. **Turn R** onto the road (signed Letcombe Bassett) and carefully descend the steep hill into the village. **Turn L** at the T-junction in the village (signed Childrey/Lambourn) and leave the village up a short sharp hill. **Turn R** at the next T-junction (signed

Letcombe Regis

Wantage/Childrey) and go straight ahead at the crossroads with the B4507 and descend gently into Childrey. **Turn R** by the Hatchett pub (Stow Hill).

Turn up a tarmac bridlepath between houses (signed as a No Through Road) and climb gently. Go straight across, still on a track where it crosses the minor road. Enter East Challow passing a school on your left and **turn R** onto Windmill Place. Take the second **turn L** (High View) and **turn R** at the T-junction opposite the cricket ground (Vicarage Hill). **Turn L** back onto the B4507 (not signed) and coast gently down into Wantage.

Turn L onto Ham Road (signed Oxford/Grove A338) and soon **turn R** onto Locks Lane. Descend carefully as

there is a deep ford at the bottom. Cross the ford on the footbridge and continue up Locks Lane following the one-way system. **Turn L** onto Portway. The turning to the car park is soon on your left. To return to the Market Square, follow Portway and **turn L** at the traffic lights (signed Town Centre, etc.) and follow the road back to the square.

● ● ● ● ● ● ● ● ● ● ● ● ● ● ● ● ● ● ● ●

THE RIDGEWAY

The Ridgeway has been described as the 'greatest, lengthiest and noblest in appearance of all prehistoric roads'. It may well be among the oldest roads in the world. Today its status is byway not bridlepath, reflecting its ancient usage. It runs along one of the six ridges that radiate from Salisbury Plain, through Wiltshire, Oxfordshire and Berkshire. All

The defence ditch at Segsbury Castle

along its length there is ample evidence of the prehistoric people who first trod it. There are earthworks aplenty, hill forts and the beautiful and ancient chalk hill figure, the Uffington White Horse.

SEGSBURY HILL FORT

The Segsbury hill fort has an extensive ditch and rampart system with four 'gateways'. The site was first excavated in 1871 by a Dr Phene. He discovered a cist grave on the south side of the hill fort rampart. The grave was floored with stone slabs and the sides were walled with flint. Finds included a shield boss and fragments of an urn or drinking cup. Among other finds were human bones and flint scrapers and it has been suggested that this was a secondary Anglo-Saxon burial. Reuse of an ancient site for such a purpose is not unusual. A more recent excavation by archaeologists from Oxford University carried out in 1996 and 1997 suggested that the fort was used periodically between the 6th and 2nd centuries BC, possibly as a communal centre for various activities, including sheep management and exchange.

17
Goring: Riding through the Gap
15 miles

This route may not be long in miles, but it certainly gives riders the full 'Chilterns experience'! As you cycle, you will see all the features typical of this part of the country: dry valleys, beech and yew woodland, flint and brick buildings and, of course, the River Thames. The ride heads east out of Goring, climbing steadily for about 2 miles up a dry valley, passing Elvendon Priory before reaching the village of Woodcote. We then turn back towards the river, coasting gently through beech woodlands to the village of Mapledurham with its Tudor house and watermill. Film buffs amongst you may recognise it as the setting for the film *The Eagle has Landed*. The route continues along a short section of bridle track before emerging onto a gravel road through the beautiful riverside Hardwick estate. At Whitchurch you have a choice of route. Either you can climb Whitchurch Hill on-road and return to Goring via Cray's Pond or you can opt for the more scenic and definitely more exciting off-road option which takes the Thames Path as far as Gatehampton Manor.

Maps: OS Landranger 175 Reading and Windsor, plus OS Explorer 171 which is useful for those riding the off-road route (GR SU602807).

Starting point: Goring is located on the River Thames, some 10 miles north-west of Reading. The route starts and finishes outside the railway station, which is on Gatehampton Road on the east side of the railway line from London (Paddington) to Reading and Oxford. There is a regular stopping train service between Ealing Broadway and Oxford on which bikes may be taken without a reservation. If arriving by car, there is a long-term car park on Station Road (to the west of the railway line). To find it, go down the High Street and follow the parking sign to the east along Manor Road and into Station Road. The entrance to the car park is immediately beyond the Catherine Wheel pub.

Refreshments: There are several pubs which serve food in Goring, including the Catherine Wheel in Station Road and the John Barleycorn in Manor Road. If you prefer to picnic, there is a riverside picnic area at Mapledurham Mill or plenty of benches in the nearby churchyard. Alternatively Hartslock Wood, with its spectacular views down to the River Thames, is also a good place to choose.

The route: This is a fantastic ride. However, it shouldn't be undertaken if you are riding a bike with very narrow tyres or a very heavy or laden bike, or are pulling a trailer or tag-along. Please take care to look out for walkers and push your bike if you don't feel confident to ride.

A tranquil stretch of the Thames

If you are starting from the car park, ride out past the Catherine Wheel public house and **turn L**. Soon **bear L** (Red Cross Road) and **turn R** at the T-junction with the High Street to cross the railway bridge. **Turn L** onto the route (signed Crowmarsh/Wallingford B4009).

Otherwise leave the railway station and **turn L**. Keep straight on, with the railway bridge on your left (signed Crowmarsh/Wallingford B4009). **Turn R** along Elvedon Road (signed Woodcote/Ipsden) and keep on this road following signs for Woodcote. The road climbs steadily up a dry valley, passing the Elvendon Priory. Go straight on at the crossroads (signed Shirvells Hill) and continue climbing. **Turn R** at the T-junction onto Long Toll (not signed). The next junction is

complicated, but keep more or less straight ahead and to your left, following the sign for Goring Heath. Keep on this road following signs to Mapledurham. After just over 2½ miles, **turn R** at the crossroads, following the brown sign to Mapledurham House and Mill (No Through Road). Follow this road into the village. The entrance to the House and Mill are at the end of the road, near the church.

When you are ready to leave, retrace your steps back up the road for about ¼ mile. **Turn L** along a bridle track on a left-hand bend in the road by a white cottage (signed Whitchurch/Chiltern Way Extension). After a little over ½ mile ride through some iron gates onto a gravel road through the Hardwick estate. Exit the estate through similar gates and go straight ahead onto the

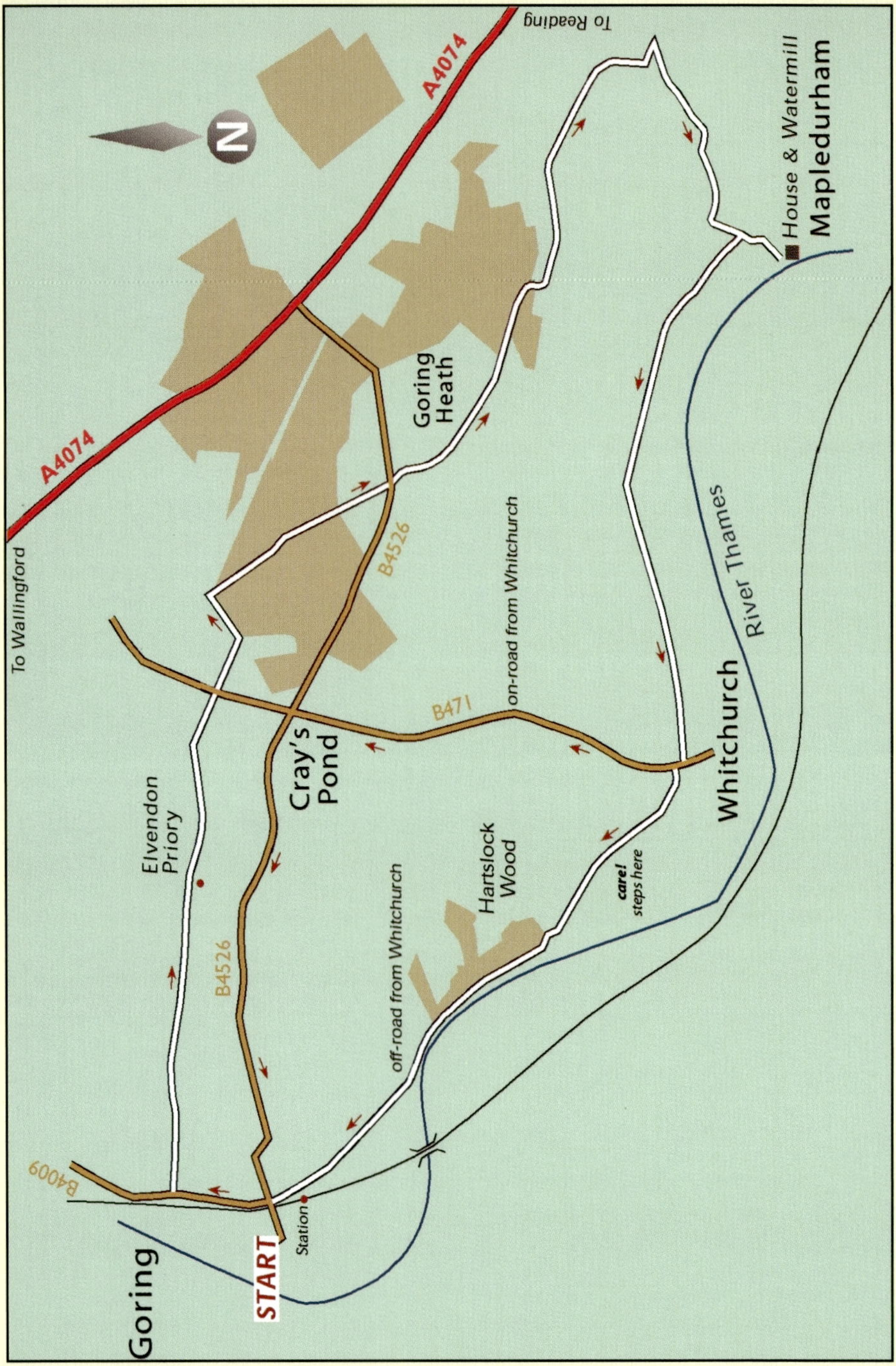

To Reading

A4074

House & Watermill
Mapledurham

N

A4074

Goring Heath

B4526

To Wallingford

River Thames

B471

on-road from Whitchurch

Cray's Pond

Whitchurch

Elvendon Priory

Hartslock Wood

B4526

care!
steps here

off-road from Whitchurch

B4009

Goring

START

Station

tarmac road (signed Whitchurch). In Whitchurch, **turn R** at the T-junction (signed Goring Heath/Woodcote). Now you have a choice:

On-road return to Goring

Keep straight on up Whitchurch Hill (B471). **Turn L** after about 2 miles at the T-junction (or staggered crossroads) in Cray's Pond (signed Goring B4526). **Turn L** at the T-junction in Goring to return to the station, or **turn R** and then **turn L** over the railway bridge to return to Goring itself.

Off-road return to Goring

Soon **turn L** (signed Thames Path/Hartslock bridle track) and ride along the road through the Coombe Park estate. When the tarmac road runs out, get off your bike and push it carefully down and up the steps crossing a narrow dry valley. DO NOT ATTEMPT TO RIDE THIS SECTION! Once past this the track goes into Hartslock Wood, a fantastic beech and yew woodland. The track is narrow in places but has a good solid surface and should give you an exhilarating ride as long as you exercise caution on the occasional steep section. If in doubt, get off and walk and take the opportunity to enjoy the view down to the river and the sights and smells of the woods. After a mile or so you will emerge on a concrete road. Keep straight ahead (signed Goring). **Turn L** at the T-junction (not signed) and soon you will see the railway station on your left. To return to the centre of Goring, ride past the station and **turn L** over the railway bridge.

● ●

GORING

Goring is now a small thriving town of some 3,500 inhabitants on the north bank of the River Thames within the Goring Gap, which divides the Chiltern Hills (to the east) from the Berkshire Downs (to the west). Although both prehistoric and Roman artefacts have been found in the area, it is thought that Goring was redeveloped in the Saxon period. It appears in the Domesday Book as Goringes and was valued at £15, somewhat less than its neighbour on the opposite bank of the Thames, Streatley (valued at £24). It continued to exist in Streatley's shadow until 1840 when the coming of the railway and the building of the station led to much expansion and the building of many riverside villas. The Thames itself was crossed here only by ferry until the first road bridge was built to link the two settlements in 1837.

MAPLEDURHAM HOUSE AND WATERMILL

As you descend down into the tiny Thames-side village of Mapledurham you will find that it still exudes a feudal air. At the end of the road is the entrance to Mapledurham House and Watermill, both of which are open to the public on weekend and bank holiday afternoons from April to the end of September, and Sundays in October. The house is one of the largest Tudor houses in the country and still retains a good amount of original detail despite restorations in the late 18th and early 19th centuries. Construction of the present house was begun around 1585 by Sir Richard Blount and it is still owned by one of his descendants. Its typically Tudor brick diaperwork exterior is supposed to have been the inspiration for Kenneth Grahame's Toad Hall.

There has been a watermill nearby on the River Thames since at least the time of the Domesday Book, although the present building has a core which dates to the 15th century. It is now the only working mill on the Thames.

Wallingford: Rivers Great and Small

22 miles

This route heads north from Wallingford to cross the River Thames at Shillingford before visiting Dorchester on the other side of the River Thame. It wends its way back to Wallingford through the pleasant villages of Drayton St Leonard, Berrick Salome, Chalgrove, Ewelme and Benson before crossing the old town bridge. There is plenty to see and visit along the way. You can taste and buy locally produced wines at the Brightwell Vineyard (along the road to Shillingford Bridge, open weekends), explore the historic town of Dorchester with its abbey, museum and old coaching inns, or visit the Newington Nursery (on the A329 north of Newington) which specialises in hardy exotic plants, including orchids. Alternatively, relax beside a river at Ewelme watercress beds or Preston Crowmarsh lock and weir. You can always flop down in the Castle Meadows back in Wallingford at the end of your ride.

Maps: OS Landranger 175 Reading and Windsor and 164 Oxford, Chipping Norton and Bicester (GR SU607895).

Starting point: The route starts from the crossroads in the centre of Wallingford, where High Street meets Castle Street and St Martin's Street. Wallingford is located on the River Thames, 15 miles south-east of Oxford or 12 miles north-west of Reading. The nearest railway stations are Didcot or Appleford (both about 6 miles away). There is a convenient car park (pay and display) on Castle Street; turn R out of the car park and you are on the route.

Refreshments: Wallingford has plenty of pubs for refreshments. In the summer there is a regular refreshment kiosk in the park by the bridge. The Red Lion at Chalgrove, the Waterfront Café at Benson and the Abbey Tea Rooms at Dorchester are all popular venues with local cyclists. Newington Nursery also has a tea room where you can relax surrounded by tropical plants, a good choice if the weather is cool!

The route: This route is gently undulating with just a couple of very short hills.

Start by heading north along Castle Street. There is a small car park and an entrance to the Castle Meadows shortly on your right. Continue for about 1½ miles before descending to traffic lights at Shillingford Bridge. Cross the bridge and continue to the A4074 at a roundabout. Get onto the pavement cycle track heading to your left on the far side of the road (signed Oxford/Dorchester). The easiest way to do this is to dismount and push your bike along the footway and cross the A4074 using the traffic island. Ride

To Thame

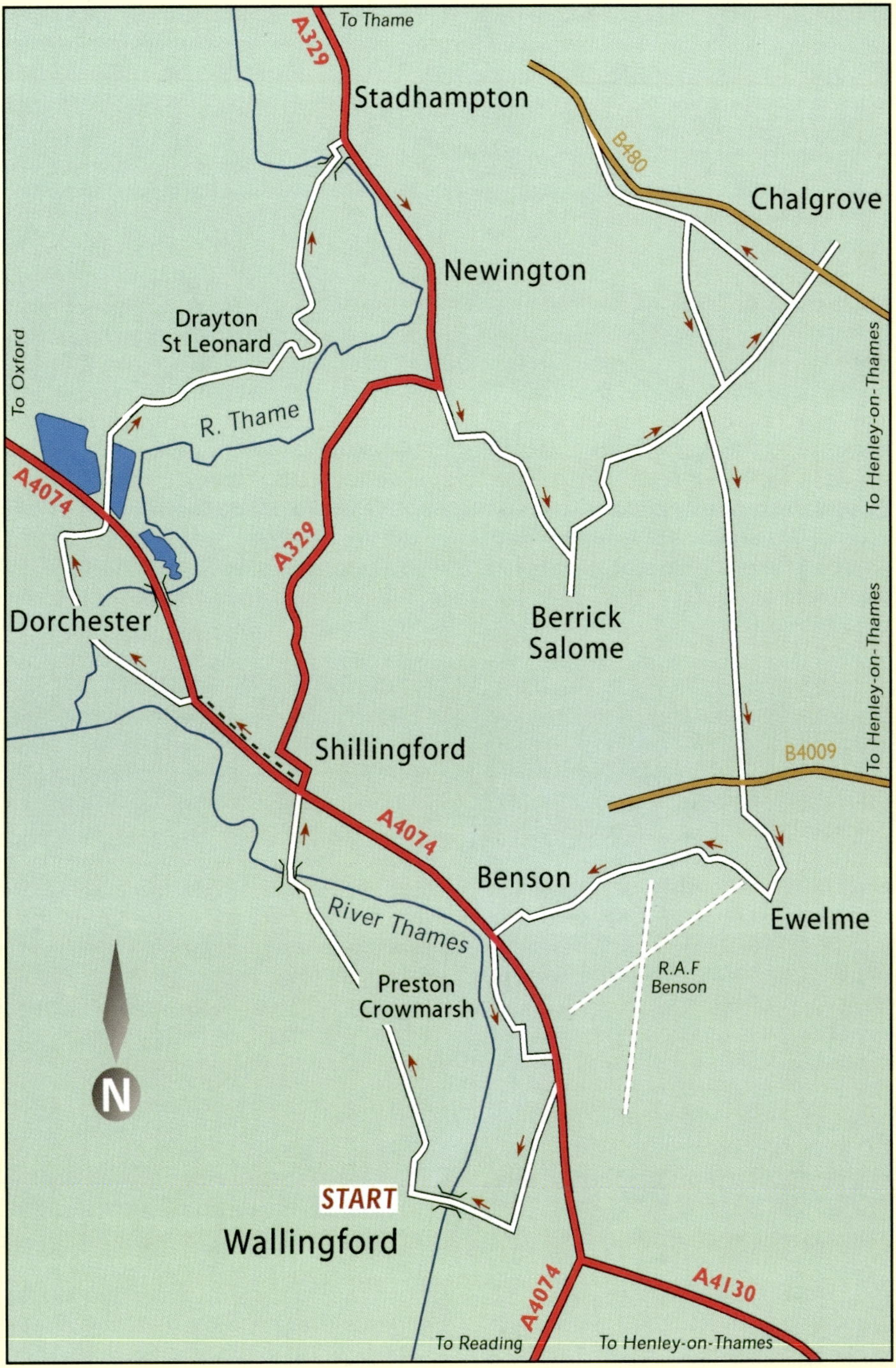

A329

Stadhampton

B480

Chalgrove

Newington

Drayton
St Leonard

R. Thame

To Oxford

A4074

A329

Dorchester

Berrick
Salome

To Henley-on-Thames

To Henley-on-Thames

B4009

Shillingford

A4074

Benson

Ewelme

River Thames

Preston
Crowmarsh

R.A.F
Benson

N

START

Wallingford

A4074

A4130

To Reading

To Henley-on-Thames

along the track with care because the surface is uneven in places with the occasional kerb. Also visibility can be restricted by foliage! After approximately ¾ mile, cross the A4074 using the traffic island provided. Follow the track ahead and to your right and soon **turn L** onto the road to Dorchester.

Cross the River Thame on the stone bridge and enter Dorchester along the High Street. A short distance along is the George Hotel (an old coaching inn), and opposite is the lych gate entrance to Dorchester Abbey and Museum which are well worth a visit, especially at times when the tea room is open! When you are ready, continue along the High Street and **turn R** at a crossroads at the far end of the village into Drayton Road (not signed).

Cross the A4074 on a bridge providing access to Queenford Farm. At the far end, just before the crash barrier **turn L** onto the footpath/cycleway. The pavement has not been let down, so take care. Also take care on the descent and the sharp bends. Once parallel with the A4074, **turn R** between two sections of hedge onto a narrow path which leads into the end of a road (not signed). You will soon see that there are flooded gravel pits on either side. Proceed along this road and **turn R** at the T-junction (not signed). Ride through Drayton St Leonard, following signs for Stadhampton. Beyond the village the road runs next to the River Thame and is prone to flooding. Should you encounter floods, there is a section of raised walkway that you can push your bike along. Ride to the T-junction with the A329 and **turn R** (not signed).

Ride through Newington, where you will sometimes see sheep being used as 'green lawnmowers' in the churchyard. Beyond the village there is a short climb. **Turn L** at the top (signed Berrick Salome). **Turn L** on the outskirts of the village (signed Chalgrove/Watlington). Soon after entering Chalgrove, **turn L** at the junction with a bridge and triangle of grass (signed Stadhampton/ Oxford). The Red Lion pub is soon on your right and there are many historic old buildings. There is a brook running alongside the road and sometimes ducks come up onto the road. This is the best 'traffic calming' one can get! Take care in case they make an unexpected appearance. If you wish to visit the church to look at the medieval wall paintings, then **turn L** down Church Lane. When you have explored adequately, continue along High Street and **turn L** (signed Berrick Salome/Benson).

Turn R at the T-junction (signed Berrick Salome/Benson). Soon **turn L** (signed Ewelme). Go straight ahead at the crossroads with the B4009 (not signed). **Turn R** at the following T-junction (also not signed) and ride into Ewelme. **Turn R** at the T-junction (pub on left-hand side, signed RAF Benson/Wallingford). Cross the stream and watercress beds and **bear R** (signed Benson/Oxford) passing alongside Benson aerodrome until you enter Benson itself.

Keep on this road through the village and **turn L** at the war memorial (signed Crowmarsh/Wallingford). Very close to the T-junction with the main road, **turn R** onto the footpath/cycleway. Cross the A4074 using the traffic island and **turn L** along a short section of pathway. **Turn R** (not signed) to ride

Cress beds at Ewelme

through Preston Crowmarsh. Look out for a sign for the Thames Path on your right. This leads down to Preston Crowmarsh lock and weir over the River Thames, a lovely spot for a rest or a picnic (bikes should be pushed across the bridge and weir).

Turn **R** at the T-junction with the main road, onto the footpath/cycleway and soon **turn R** again (not signed). This road used to be the main road out of Wallingford but is now much quieter. Turn **R** at the mini-roundabout at the end of this road (signed Wallingford).

One of the rows of black and white terraced cottages on your right, shortly before the town bridge, sports a blue plaque commemorating Jethro Tull (1674–1741), who invented the horse-drawn seed drill. The seed drill is still in use today, but now drawn by tractor. Ride over the River Thames and back to the start in the centre of Wallingford.

WALLINGFORD

Wallingford started life as a fortified Saxon town or burgh. William the Conqueror forded the Thames here after the battle of Hastings and the motte and bailey castle was one of the first to be built after the invasion, in 1071. Wallingford was a staunch Royalist stronghold in the Civil War which explains why, afterwards, Oliver Cromwell was so keen to destroy the castle. Now all that remains are a few walls and some impressive earthworks, forming part of the wonderfully tranquil Castle Gardens whose entrance is next to the Castle Street car park. It's a lovely place for a picnic or just to relax after your ride.

The first bridge over the Thames was built in 1141. The present 19-arch bridge spans 900 ft of river and water meadow. The Wallingford Museum, on High Street, is worth visiting and includes a time-warp walk through Saxon and medieval Wallingford with personal audio commentary. The museum is open all year till 30th November, Tuesday to Friday 2 pm to 5 pm and Saturday 10.30 am to 5 pm, and June to August it is also open Sundays 2 pm to 5 pm. There is an admission charge.

EWELME

Ewelme is a pleasant brick and flint village. Its name means spring or source of water, and it's not difficult to understand why, as a crystal clear stream flows through the village feeding watercress beds. The current beds were built around 1925 and were in commercial operation until 1965. They are now a local nature reserve where, if you are very lucky, you may see a water vole. Take some time to explore the scenic church and adjoining medieval school and almshouses. This was a classic combination of buildings which rarely survive to the modern day intact. They were founded by Alice Chaucer, granddaughter of the poet and wife of the Duke of Suffolk. The churchyard contains the grave of Jerome K. Jerome whose tale *Three Men in a Boat* still epitomises leisure time on the Thames.

DORCHESTER

Dorchester has been an important Christian centre since the missionary Bishop Birinus (later saint) baptised Cynegils, pagan King of Wessex, here in AD 635. The present abbey church is thought to have been built on the site of the original Saxon abbey. It once held the shrine to St Birinus and was an important place of pilgrimage in the 13th and 14th centuries. Like so many, it did not survive the dissolution unscathed. However, thanks to the generosity of Richard Beauforest, the abbey church was bought for the continued use of the parish. It is a pleasure to wander through its tranquil aisles, admiring the stained glass and sculptured tombs.

Watlington: A Trip to Red Kite Country

6½ and 10½ miles

Watlington is a small market town sitting under the Chilterns escarpment. The older part of the town contains many interesting buildings, although like many small towns it has changed in character over the last few decades. The route explores some of the quiet villages that lie at the bottom of the Chiltern escarpment to the north. In recent years this area has become the centre of the reintroduced red kite population. The birds nest in many of the woodlands and can often be seen flying low over both Watlington and the surrounding villages.

Maps: OS Landranger 165 Aylesbury and Leighton Buzzard, and 175 Reading and Windsor (GR SU690945).

Starting point: The ride starts and finishes at the town hall, which is located at the end of Couching Street. There is a large free car park a short distance from the start, in Hill Road. It is signposted from the centre of Watlington. Alternatively, if you have a folding bicycle, you can use the regular bus service (No 101, Thames Travel) which runs between Oxford and Watlington (Monday to Saturday). This service terminates at Watlington public library.

Refreshments: There are several pubs in Watlington. Around the route, the Half Moon pub in Cuxham serves food.

The route: This ride has two loops. The start and finish of the loops are the same but the outer parts will give you the choice of a shorter or longer ride. The out-going route is on the B4009 and is the busiest road along either route. They are both gently undulating.

6½-mile route
Head north from the town hall into Shirburn Street and out of town on the B4009. After approximately ½ mile, **turn L** (signed Pyrton). Cycle through the village and then up a small hill (Clare Hill). **Turn L** at the crossroads (signed Cuxham/Brightwell). Now you are rewarded with a downhill stretch of road and great views over towards the Chiltern Hills. Carry on till you reach the T-junction with the B480. **Turn L** (signed Brightwell/Cuxham/ Watlington) and ride through the village of Cuxham. Continue following the B480 back into Watlington. On entering Watlington go straight ahead at the mini-roundabout. **Bear L** at the junction with the B4009 (CARE!). **Turn L** into Couching Street where the town hall is situated.

10½-mile route
Head north from the town hall into

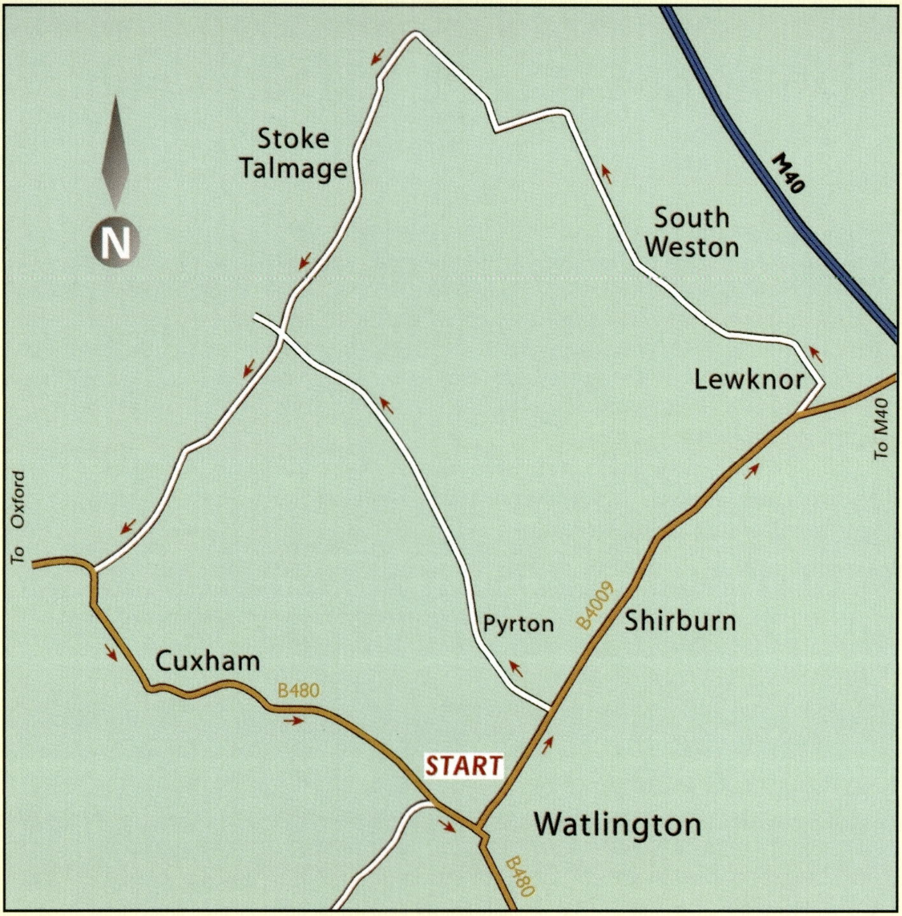

Shirburn Street and out of town on the B4009. Ride through the village of Shirburn. After about 2½ miles, **turn L** (signed Lewknor/South Weston/Adwell) and ride into the village of Lewknor. **Turn L** by the Leathern Bottle public house (signed South Weston/Adwell). Ride through South Weston. **Turn L** at the T-junction (no signpost). This road climbs steadily, passing through the edge of Stoke Talmage and on to the junction with the B480.

Turn L (signed Brightwell/Cuxham/Watlington) and ride through the

village of Cuxham. Continue following the B480 back into Watlington. On entering Watlington go straight ahead at the mini-roundabout. **Bear L** at the junction with the B4009 (CARE!). **Turn L** into Couching Street. Couching Street ends at the town hall, so completing the ride.

● ● ● ● ● ● ● ● ● ● ● ● ● ● ● ● ● ● ● ●

RED KITES
As you ride this route, you are almost certain to see the magnificent red kites soaring majestically above you. These days, tractors carrying out hay cutting or

90

In Lewknor village

ploughing are often pursued by flocks of these spectacular birds on the look out for a free meal. However, it wasn't always so. Their relationship with man has not always been a happy one. They have long been regarded as vermin, which is odd because they are primarily scavengers and rarely take live prey. In the 1860s, such was the zeal to get rid of them that a price of 1d was paid for each bird killed. They were officially exterminated from England around 1880, but managed to hold out in the more remote areas of mid Wales where, by the 1980s, their population had sunk to around 30 pairs. The decision to reintroduce them in England was taken in 1989 and the Chiltern Hills were chosen as the first reintroduction site. The project, run jointly by Natural England and RSPB, used young birds brought to the UK from Spain. These were deemed to be the closest genetically to the original English birds. It wasn't possible to use birds from the Welsh population because its numbers were still too low.

Birds were reintroduced annually for several years until breeding was established. There are now around 300 pairs in the area and chicks from the Chilterns have been used to seed new populations all over the country. Not surprisingly the project has been dubbed the greatest conservation success story of the 20th century.

WATLINGTON

Watlington's origins probably date back to the Bronze Age, but the town is first reliably recorded during Saxon times. Its town hall was built towards the latter part of the 17th century to celebrate the restoration of the monarchy. The sturdy brick arches with toothed patterning provided a covered space where a market could be held, and the rooms above were used for a grammar school. The centre of the town is full of medieval and Georgian buildings, a surprising number of which are former pubs! Today the town still retains many local shops and businesses.

Thame: Following the Phoenix

21 miles

The Chiltern Hills are never far away on this ride, but don't worry, you can admire them from the saddle without actually having to climb them. The route leaves Thame in a westerly direction and then turns south along a quiet no through road to the village of Moreton. A bridle track leads to Tetsworth, and a short detour takes you down to the village green where cricket can often be watched on Sunday afternoons and a quiet pint enjoyed. We then cross under the M40 and enjoy the lush scenery of what we like to think of as the 'foothills' of the Chilterns, and the small hamlets of Wheatfield and Adwell. Soon you will find yourself riding parallel with the Chiltern escarpment. At some point you are certain to enjoy a close encounter with a red kite, a truly spectacular and welcome reintroduction to the native fauna. After passing underneath the M40 for a second time, the route passes through Kingston Stert and on to Kingston Blount, through Chinnor and on to meet the Phoenix Trail near Hinton Crossing.

Map: OS Landranger 165 Aylesbury and Leighton Buzzard (GR SP706059).

Starting point: The town hall on Cornmarket in the centre of Thame. If arriving by car we recommend you park at the Cattle Market pay and display long-term car park on North Street (signposted and a short distance from the town centre). The nearest railway station is Haddenham and Thame Parkway which is located some 3 miles to the north-east of Thame.

Refreshments: There are plenty of pubs and cafés in Thame itself. Along the route the Old Red Lion in Tetsworth and the Cherry Tree in Kingston Blount are good for food. If you want to enjoy an outdoor picnic, there is a big village green at Tetsworth (down the hill and to your right as you reach the main road). Alternatively, there are plenty of seats along the Phoenix Trail.

The route: This ride is generally fairly flat with a few short climbs on quiet roads. In addition to the well-surfaced Phoenix Trail that can be happily ridden in all weathers, the route includes another section of bridleway between Moreton and Tetsworth. This has a gravel surface and can be tackled by any bike except after heavy rain when sections of it do hold water.

From the town hall in Thame, head in a westerly direction along the High Street. Go straight ahead at the first mini-roundabout and immediately **turn L** at the second mini-roundabout (by the Rising Sun pub). Go straight over at the next mini-roundabout and go straight ahead at the 'give way' line and **bear R** onto Windmill Road (signed Sustrans Route 57). **Turn R** at

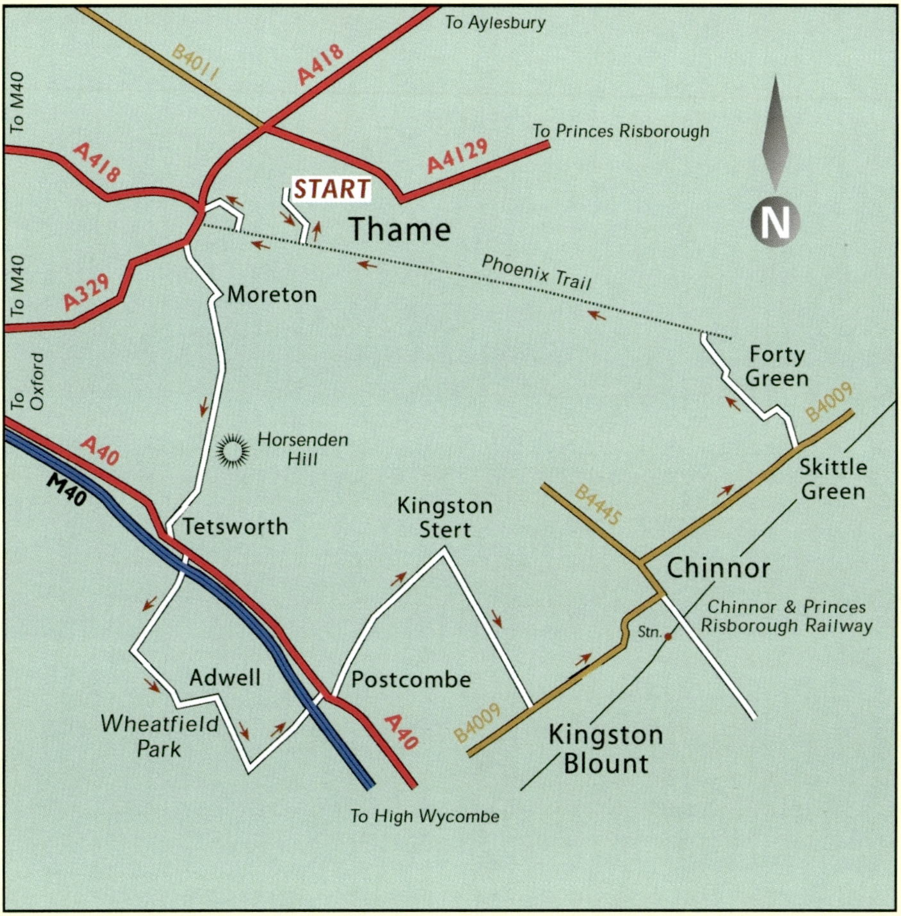

To Aylesbury

B4011

A418

To Princes Risborough

A4129

To M40

A418

START

Thame

To M40

A329

Moreton

Phoenix Trail

N

Forty
Green

B4009

To Oxford

A40

Horsenden
Hill

M40

Skittle
Green

B4445

Tetsworth

Kingston
Stert

Chinnor

Chinnor & Princes
Risborough Railway

Stn.

Adwell

Postcombe

A40

B4009

Kingston
Blount

Wheatfield
Park

To High Wycombe

the end of the road onto Route 57. After a while **bear R** on a sharp bend and ride through the barriers. This section is technically a footpath, although it is well-used by local cyclists, so take extra care to look out for pedestrians and be prepared to get off your bike if asked. Soon **turn L** through more barriers and ride with the leisure centre on your left. **Turn R** at the T-junction with the road and follow the road out of the leisure centre car park. **Turn L** onto the cycle track adjacent to the main road (signed Shabbington) and follow the

cycle track signs, emerging on Rycote Lane.

Turn L onto Rycote Lane (signed Wallingford A329, etc.). **Turn L** after mile (signed Moreton Village Only). In Moreton, **bear R** at the war memorial and soon **bear L** (signed Bridleway). For a while this remains a tarmac road, but it then changes to a rough track and climbs over Horsenden Hill before continuing into the village of Tetsworth. The pleasant pub and village green are located to your right along the main road. To continue on the

Thame High Street

route, **turn L** (not signed) and after ½ mile **turn R** (signed Stoke Talmage/ Adwell). Ride under the M40 and after a while **turn L** (signed Adwell/South Weston). Ride through the peaceful parkland scenery and, if you wish, you can make short detours to visit the church in Wheatfield Park or the tiny hamlet of Adwell.

Turn L (signed Postcombe) and soon ride underneath the M40 for a second time. In Postcombe, **turn R** (signed Stokenchurch) and immediately **turn L** (signed Chalford/Sydenham). **Turn R** into Kingston Stert (signed Kingston Blount) and ride along, towards the escarpment. Follow the road into Kingston Blount and when you reach the junction with the B4009, **turn L** (signed Chinnor/Princes Risborough). Follow this road for about 1½ miles into the small town of Chinnor.

Turn L at the mini-roundabout in Chinnor (signed Princes Risborough/Thame) and after a while **turn R** (signed Princes Risborough/ Aylesbury B4009). Continue for a mile or so and then **turn L** onto a no through road (signed Skittle Green/Forty Green). Ride for another 1½ miles, keeping left and passing through the hamlets of Skittle Green and Forty Green. Soon after passing some gates marked 'Hinton Crossing' you will meet the Phoenix Trail, which uses the path of the old railway line from Princes Risborough to Thame. **Turn L** onto the Phoenix Trail (signed Thame) and follow the path, taking care at road crossings, till you return to where you originally joined the track at the bottom of Windmill Road in Thame. **Turn R** along Windmill Road (signed Town Centre). **Bear L** at the end of the road (not signed) and go

On the Phoenix Trail

straight over the mini-roundabout and ride with the recreation ground on your left. **Turn R** at the mini-roundabout by the Rising Sun pub and go straight over the next mini-roundabout to return to the town hall in Thame.

● ●

THAME

Thame is a bustling market town with twice-weekly cattle markets and a street market on a Tuesday in its spacious, boat-shaped market place. The original town developed around the church, but in the 13th century a new town was 'planted' on virgin land around the current market place by the Bishop of Lincoln, who was so keen to have the market patronised that he actually diverted the road from Aylesbury to ensure that travellers passed by. The modern market square still retains some lovely old buildings, such as the

Birdcage pub which is reputed to date from around 1300. Like so many towns and villages in this part of Oxfordshire, it has strong Civil War connections. In fact during that time it was a kind of no-man's-land occupied at various stage by either side. John Hampden, the famed Parliamentarian, was educated at Thame and died there in 1643 of wounds sustained while holding out against the superior forces of Prince Rupert at the battle of Chalgrove Field.

CHINNOR AND PRINCES RISBOROUGH RAILWAY

The history of this small branch line, which originally carried trains the 8 miles and 66 chains from the Great Western Station at Princes Risborough to a terminus at Pyrton, just outside Watlington, is a depressingly familiar one for train lovers everywhere. It was authorised by an Act of Parliament in 1869 and its construction was paid for by local businessmen. However, it immediately ran into financial problems after its opening in 1872 and was eventually sold to GWR in 1883 for about half the sum it cost to build! Like many small local railways, passenger traffic dropped off steadily and it was shut for all but freight in 1957. Sections of track were removed, but some remained to offer a freight service to the nearby cement works. Even this stopped in 1989. The Chinnor and Princes Risborough Railway Association took responsibility for the section from Chinnor eastwards to the Thame branch in 1990 and they operate up to 5 trains per day at weekends (see www.chinnorrailway.co.uk for the current timetable and ticket prices). They are located on Hill Road. From the route in Chinnor, **turn R** at the junction of the B4009 and the B4445 (Station Road).

FURTHER INFORMATION ABOUT CYCLING IN THE OXFORDSHIRE AREA

The Cyclists' Touring Club is the national organisation which represents and campaigns for the interests of all cyclists, whether they ride to work or ride around the world. The club has touring and technical departments to help with all your cycling queries, and issues a bi-monthly magazine to its members. In the Oxfordshire area there are also local CTC groups which organise a variety of day and half-day rides. All these groups welcome new riders. Rides are led by experienced local cyclists on quiet country roads. If you have enjoyed the rides in this book, why not make contact with your local group and ride with like-minded people? A list of contacts in the region covered by this book is given below. Alternatively, there are local groups all over the country, so if you are not local, why not contact the CTC direct to find about groups in your area?

Finally we would both like to thank all our friends in the Oxfordshire CTC, not only for their help riding the routes in this book and their polite enquiries about its progress, but also for their unfailing friendship over the years and for all the expertise and confidence that we have picked up through riding with them.

LOCAL CYCLING GROUPS

Oxfordshire CTC Members Group
Website: www.oxonctc.org.uk
Oxford: James (telephone: 01865 327969)
Witney: Kevin (telephone: 01993 700837)
Wantage: Glen (telephone: 01235 768428) or sec@ctcwantage.org.uk

Isis Cyclists (short rides for women in Oxford):
    http://isiscyclistsctc.wordpress.com

Reading CTC
Website: www.readingctc.co.uk
John (telephone: 07818 400440) or secretary@readingctc.co.uk

CTC South Bucks
Telephone: 01494 815642
Email: baldrick@southbuckscycling.org.uk

CTC (Cyclists' Touring Club) National Headquarters
Website: www.ctc.org.uk
Telephone: 01483 238337
Email: Cycling@ctc.org.uk